Haydn: The 'Paris' Symphonies

Haydn's Symphonies Nos. 82–7 are seminal works in Haydn's output and mark a new level of compositional attainment, launching the important cycle of mature Haydn symphonies written for an international audience. Three chapters of the book deal with the reception of Haydn's symphonies in Paris, documenting the extent to which they dominated the repertoire of important public concert series. The aesthetic basis of Haydn's reception in Paris in the 1780s is considered in discussions of the notions of 'popular' and 'learned' taste, and such notions inform the commentaries on the symphonies themselves. Thus as well as discussing technical features of Symphonies Nos. 82–7, broader concerns include the relationship between orchestral splendour and eighteenth-century notions of beauty; the relationship between genius, originality and convention; irony and humour, and the updating of popular orchestral taste.

BERNARD HARRISON is Head of the Music Department at Lancaster University. His publications include *A Catalogue of Contemporary Irish Music* (Dublin, 1982) and *Haydn's Keyboard Music: Studies in Performance Practice* (Oxford, 1997).

CAMBRIDGE MUSIC HANDBOOKS

GENERAL EDITOR Julian Rushton

Haydn: The 'Paris' Symphonies

Bernard Harrison

CAMBRIDGE
UNIVERSITY PRESS

PUBLISHED BY THE PRESS SYNDICATE OF THE UNIVERSITY OF CAMBRIDGE
The Pitt Building, Trumpington Street, Cambridge CB2 1RP

CAMBRIDGE UNIVERSITY PRESS
The Edinburgh Building, Cambridge CB2 2RU, United Kingdom
40 West 20th Street, New York, NY 10011–4211, USA
10 Stamford Road, Oakleigh, Melbourne 3166, Australia

First published 1998

Printed in the United Kingdom at the University Press, Cambridge

Typeset in Ehrhardt MT 10½/13pt, in QuarkXPress™ [SE]

A catalogue record for this book is available from the British Library

Library of Congress cataloguing in publication data
Harrison, Bernard.
Haydn, the 'Paris' symphonies / Bernard Harrison.
p.   cm. – (Cambridge music handbooks)
Includes bibliographical references and index.
ISBN 0 521 47164 8 (hardback) – ISBN 0 521 47743 3 (paperback)
1. Haydn, Joseph, 1732–1809.   Symphonies, – I, 82–87.
2. Symphony – 18th century.   I. Title.   II. Series.
ML410.H4H314   1998
784.2′184′092–dc21   97–42606   CIP MN

ISBN 0 521 47164 8 hardback
ISBN 0 521 47743 3 paperback

Contents

Acknowledgements

In the writing of this book I have been lucky to benefit from the help and advice of a number of friends and colleagues. Michael Fend kindly commented on drafts of a large part of this book and, over a number of years, has generously shared ideas with me which have been influential in my thinking. Mary O'Neill has been a scrupulous and imaginative adviser on problems of translation, and her experience with French sources saved me much time at the earlier stages in the research for this book. Julian Rushton has been a sympathetic and meticulous editor, whose comments have saved me from many minor embarrassments and the reader from a more self-indulgent book. I am grateful to him and to Penny Souster for their interest in the subject and for their gentle reminders of the passing of time. Neil Boynton read Chapter 5 with his customary care, and it is a pleasure to acknowledge the perceptive and helpful copy-editing of Eric Van Tassel.

I am also grateful to various cohorts of undergraduate and postgraduate students who have endured earlier and formative versions of what follows and who helped me, sometimes unwittingly, to clarify ideas. I am particularly indebted to Abigail Chantler for her reading of various drafts and for helpful discussions on broader questions of eighteenth-century aesthetics.

In preparing this book I have been heavily and happily reliant on the resources of the Bibliothèque Nationale, Paris, and the British Library, London, and I am, as ever, grateful for the help and courtesy of the staff of both libraries.

1

Introduction

The six 'Paris' Symphonies, Nos. 82–7, composed in 1785–6,[1] were the product of a prestigious foreign commission, and like most of Haydn's music from the mid 1780s onwards they received immediate and widespread circulation throughout Europe. The commission, by the directors of the *Concert de la Loge Olympique*, was probably mooted in 1784,[2] at the instigation of Claude-François-Marie Rigoley, Comte d'Ogny, and negotiated by le Chevalier Joseph-Boulogne de Saint-Georges. The Comte d'Ogny had been a co-founder of the prestigious new concert series in 1781, an important satellite of the masonic *Loge et Société Olympique*, the principal aim of which was 'to cultivate music, and to give excellent concerts to replace those of amateurs', that is, the famous earlier *Concert des amateurs*, disbanded in January 1781 for financial reasons.[3] The choice of Haydn for the commission of 1784 built on an existing tradition of performing Haydn's symphonies at the *Concert des amateurs*, and the high profile of the new commission is reflected in the extravagant fee paid to Haydn. This was later reported as 25 *louis d'or* per symphony, with a further 5 *louis d'or* for publication rights; even excluding publication rights, it was five times the fee paid to Mozart in 1778 by Le Gros and the *Concert spirituel* for his 'Paris' Symphony, K. 297. The relationship between Haydn, the Comte d'Ogny, and the *Concert de la Loge Olympique* was to bear further fruit in 1788–9 with the commission of Symphonies Nos. 90–2.[4]

The publication history of Symphonies Nos. 82–7 is also representative of the new international dimension to Haydn's career. The rapidity with which prints of the symphonies appeared in Paris, Vienna and London in 1787–8 is an important measure of the increasing demand for Haydn's works, and Haydn's dealings with the publishers of these symphonies mark, as it were, the emergence of the composer in the marketplace. The authorised French print of the symphonies was the Imbault edition, which appeared in January 1788, and both the announcement of publication in the *Mercure de France* and the title page of the edition are headed 'From the Repertoire of the Loge Olympique' and have the claim to authority that they were 'engraved after the original scores belonging to the Loge Olympique'.[5] However, notwithstanding the fact that the rights to publication were purchased as part of the commission, Haydn also sold the works to Artaria in Vienna and Forster in London. The Artaria edition in fact appeared before the Imbault print, in December 1787, and extant correspondence from April and May of 1787 makes clear that Haydn promised Artaria sole rights in the works.[6] Haydn then wrote to Forster on 8 August 1787 offering 'six Quartets and six Symphonies, which I have not yet given to anyone' and asking a fee of 25 guineas for all twelve works.[7] Haydn's promise to Forster on 20 September 1787 that 'I shall not fail to send you the six Symphonies at the first opportunity'[8] was met by the dispatch of authentic manuscript copies of the symphonies (now British Library, Egerton 2379); thus Forster's edition of 1788 is the last of three authorised authentic editions, for each of which Haydn abstracted considerable fees while promising exclusive rights in the works. Maximising his personal gain from the symphonies, Haydn also sent copies of the symphonies gratis to Friedrich Wilhelm II, King of Prussia, and received a ring as a mark of the King's 'satisfaction and . . . favour'.[9]

Haydn was undoubtedly guilty of sharp practice, if not outright dishonesty, in his dealings with publishers over Symphonies Nos. 82–7. Similar or even more questionable dealings accompanied the commission or publication of other works in the 1780s. The most embarrassing to Haydn's reputation was undoubtedly his sale to Forster of two keyboard trios, Hob. XV:3–4, actually written by Pleyel, but duplicity was also involved in Haydn's dealings with Forster and Artaria over the publication of the Op. 50 string quartets, and Symphonies Nos. 90–2 were used to fulfil commissions to both the Comte d'Ogny and Prince Krafft Ernst von Oettingen-Wallerstein.

Haydn became in these years quite adept at deflecting personal blame, pleading mitigating circumstances, or promising future recompense when such deceptions were unveiled.[10] Whatever the rights and wrongs of Haydn's dealings with individuals, from the 1780s he effectively put in place an informal system of dual publication, whereby he benefited at least from two fees, usually from London and Vienna, for most new works produced. In so doing, Haydn took an innovatory stance in a world which traditionally favoured the publisher rather than the composer.

In the case of the 'Paris' Symphonies, although Haydn profited by sharp practice from three fees, he would have derived no benefit from the large number of prints of these symphonies which immediately followed the appearance of the first editions in Vienna, Paris and London. Even before the end of 1788, prints of orchestral parts by Hummel, Sieber, and Longman & Broderip had appeared, and in various guises the symphonies remained available in numerous new editions and reprints well into the nineteenth century. An important part of this dissemination, and a significant way in which the European musical public got to know the 'Paris' Symphonies, was in arrangements for chamber music groupings of various types. Again, this dissemination of the symphonies as domestic music happened with remarkable speed. In 1788 alone arrangements for keyboard trios and quartet (Boyé & Le Menu), for string quartet (Artaria),[11] and for keyboard and violin (Longman & Broderip)[12] had appeared and these heralded a host of similar arrangements which appeared regularly into the 1790s and beyond.[13]

The performance history of the 'Paris' Symphonies also reflects the new European context of Haydn's music in the 1780s. As argued below, in 1787–8 they were performed in Paris at the *Concert de la Loge Olympique* and the *Concert spirituel* and contributed to a peak of enthusiasm for Haydn's symphonies in Paris. It is also clear that these works were quickly introduced into the repertoires of public concerts in London: for instance, a re-issue of Symphony No. 82 by Longman & Broderip mentions performances at the Hanover Square Rooms in 1789.[14] The performance context in Paris and London would, of course, have been radically different from that at Eszterháza, and the orchestra involved would have been considerably larger than the Esterházy band or the normal court orchestra of the eighteenth century. While in the 1780s one of Joseph Le Gros's reforms of the *Concert spirituel* involved a reduction in the size of the orchestra, in 1787–8 there would still have been a contingent of approximately 56 players.[15] In 1786 the orchestra of the *Société Olympique* could call on a membership of up to 65 players (3222/4200/1/strings (14.14.7.10.4)), a mix of professional and

amateurs but containing some of Paris's leading virtuosos.[16] It is clear
that not all of the members would have been employed for every performance; certainly the clarinettists would not have been required for
Haydn's 'Paris' Symphonies, and a system of rotation may have oper-
ated. None the less the first performances of the 'Paris' Symphonies
would have been equal in scale to those of the later 'London' Symphonies by Salomon's band of about 60 players.

The 'Paris' Symphonies are fully representative of the late eighteenth-century Haydn cult, which acknowledged Haydn's status as a
genius and saw an enhancement in the esteem of instrumental music in
general and the German symphony in particular. It is one of the happy
coincidences of the last decades of the eighteenth century that Haydn's
mature symphonic style became the universal representation of the new
status of the public symphony. In them the various demands of popular
entertainment and the learned aesthetic theory of the Enlightenment
tenuously found common ground, and in each work Haydn strikes a new
and finely judged balance between a popular style and a progressive
musical language.

2

Haydn's music and the Concert spirituel

The emergence of Haydn as the dominant international symphonist in the last two decades of the eighteenth century is a major event in the history of eighteenth-century music. Haydn's two sojourns in London in the early 1790s have generally been seen as the principal exemplification of this phenomenon, and it has also been established that in the early decades of the nineteenth century Haydn's symphonies enjoyed enormous popularity with the Parisian concert-going public.[1] The rise in prominence of Haydn's symphonies in Paris in the 1780s has received less attention; and it is less well appreciated that in Paris Haydn's symphonies progressed from a relatively modest presence in public concerts in the late 1770s to dominate the Parisian symphonic repertoire to an unprecedented degree by the end of the 1780s.

The symphonic repertoire of the *Concert spirituel*, 1777–81

In tracing the increasing popularity of Haydn's symphonies in Paris the best indicator is the programming of the important concert series, the *Concert spirituel*, for which the most complete information exists.[2] The timescale under consideration is from 1777, when Haydn symphonies began to feature regularly at the *Concert spirituel*, to 1790, when the concert series came to a close. Thus the rise in popularity of Haydn's symphonies at the *Concert spirituel* takes place exactly within the directorship of Joseph Le Gros.

Haydn's symphonies were of course known in Paris before 1777. They were published in Paris, sporadically at first, from the mid 1760s and performed at the *Concert des amateurs*, and by some accounts a Haydn symphony was performed for the first time at a *Concert spirituel* in 1773.[3] If Brenet is correct in suggesting that the *Catalogue de la musique du Comte d'Ogny* represents the repertoire of the *Concert des amateurs*, then performances of Haydn symphonies must have been plentiful at this concert series before its dissolution in January 1781, since 34 symphonies attributed to Haydn (some of them falsely) are listed in the first (thematic) part of the catalogue.[4] It may well be that Le Gros inherited a close relationship in symphonic repertoire between the *Concert spirituel* and the *Concert des amateurs*.[5] Symphonies by Haydn and Gossec performed at the *Concert spirituel* in 1777, Le Gros's first season as director, were described in the *Journal de Paris* as 'du répertoire des Amateurs'.[6] A Sieber publication of symphonies by Haydn (No. 56), Gossec, and J. C. Bach, advertised in 1778, contains the description 'Les simphonies ont été joué au Concert Spirituel et au Concert des Amateurs' on the title page.[7] The same overlapping in symphonic repertoire also continued in the later 1780s between the *Concert spirituel* and the *Concert de la Loge Olympique* as witnessed in the performances of the Haydn 'Paris' Symphonies at both series.

Performances of Haydn's symphonies at the *Concert spirituel* can therefore tell only part of the story. Nevertheless, the story they tell is an interesting one. In the first five years of Le Gros's directorship of the *Concert spirituel* two earlier sources of symphonies continued to be of importance, namely, the symphonies of Mannheim composers, particularly the second generation, and the symphonies of native French composers. The Mannheim composers had provided an important part of the *Concert spirituel* repertoire since the visit of Johann Stamitz to Paris in 1754.[8] Subsequently the second generation of Mannheim composers occupied a central position in the instrumental music performed at the *Concert spirituel*, furnishing a seemingly inexhaustible supply of concertos, *symphonies concertantes*, and symphonies which for many years appears to have dominated Parisian taste in these genres.

In the symphonic repertoire of the *Concert spirituel* the two most popular second-generation Mannheim composers were Cannabich and especially Toeschi. At least one Toeschi symphony was performed in each year between 1773 and 1786, with a further single performance in 1789. Although never achieving the spectacular success of other composers, Toeschi's symphonies remained none the less a stable part of the repertoire and indeed until the early 1780s were regarded as representative of a Mannheim style which set the standards for other composers, appreciated for their charm, their fluent melody, and above all their colourful orchestration.

> [The concert of 15 August 1779] began with a symphony by Signor Toeschi. Although this piece was known already, the orchestra's performance has so to speak rejuvenated it. No other symphonist writes better than this composer. It is true that his works have a familiar air about them which sometimes approaches monotony when one compares them [with one another]; but each individual one presents a most charming picture. All his subjects, full of grace and nobility, are sustained and varied by a brilliant imagination and exquisite taste. What sets him apart from the majority of the other symphonists is above all the art of engaging the instruments in dialogue with each other, and of presenting them one after another, without ever damaging the expression or the transparency of the melody.[9]

Of the native French 'school', symphonies by Chartrain, Guénin, Navoigille, Leduc, Capron, Janson, Froment, Davaux, Candeille and others were performed regularly at the *Concert spirituel* until the early 1780s and maintained an occasional presence thereafter. Barry Brook has documented the flourishing of a French symphonic school, in the 1770s and early 1780s at least, reflected in the fact that 150 native symphonies were produced between 1768 and 1777, and 100 in the period 1778–89.[10] Gossec, who was in so many ways a seminal figure in French music in the second half of the eighteenth century,[11] was also the leading French symphonist. His symphonies were in the repertoire of the *Concert des amateurs* and the *Concert de la Loge Olympique*.[12] Although after an initial performance in 1757[13] they do not appear to feature prominently in the *Concert spirituel* until the mid 1770s, his symphonies enjoyed a sustained popularity on a par with leading foreign symphonists and were a core part of the symphonic repertoire in the early years of Le Gros's directorship.

In the first five years of Le Gros's directorship Mannheim and native French symphonies continued to be represented strongly. However, Le Gros also introduced new symphonies by three foreign composers, Haydn, Mozart, and Sterkel, in the years 1777–8. The biographical details of Mozart's unhappy visit to Paris in 1778 are well documented.[14] One of the major products of this visit was his 'Paris' Symphony (K. 297/300a), and its enthusiastic reception at the *Concert spirituel* on 18

June 1778 was reported by Mozart in a letter to his father.[15] However, Mozart's trip to Paris was only a qualified success, and, whatever the reasons, it is in any case clear that with a total of only fifteen performances of his symphonies in the period 1778–89[16] he did not become the darling of the French audiences.

It is also at least partly the case that Mozart's symphonies could not compete with the huge popularity which Sterkel's symphonies enjoyed in the *Concert spirituel* in the period 1777–82. Of the three foreign composers introduced to the concert audiences by Le Gros in 1777–8 it is initially Sterkel who enjoyed the widest popularity: in the the years 1777–82 there were 47 performances of Sterkel symphonies at the *Concert spirituel*, making his symphonies by a long way the most widely performed. Reviews of symphonies are a rarity in the eighteenth-century Parisian press, but a passing comment in the *Mercure de France* in 1779 reinforces the statistical dominance of Sterkel's symphonies of the *Concert spirituel* at this time and again hints at the reservations which reviewers held concerning Mozart's symphonies:

> The director of this Spectacle [the *Concert spirituel* of 23 May 1779], always concerned to vary the pleasures of the public, divided his concert into two parts, prefaced by two symphonies for large orchestra, one composed by Slerkel [Sterkel], whose picturesque style and beautiful harmonic effects are well known; the other by Amédeo Mozartz. Perhaps it is as learned and as majestic as the first; but it did not excite the same interest.[17]

Between 1777 and 1781 Haydn's symphonies also became established in Le Gros's repertoire, receiving from one to five performances in each year but, initially, in no way challenging Sterkel's dominance of the symphonic repertoire in the *Concert spirituel*. His music is mentioned relatively frequently in concert reports in the *Mercure de France* for the first time in 1778–9. For the most part the reviewers note the generally positive reaction to a Haydn symphony,[18] or the merits of a particular performance, or of the choice of programme.[19] Occasionally reservations were expressed concerning the difficulty of Haydn's music, particularly it seems his finales:

> The concert performed at the Château des Tuileries on Ascension Day began with a new symphony by Hayden. The first movement, of sombre

character, seemed very expressive; the second, although imitating the old French style, still gave pleasure; the third did not have the same success, because of the incoherence of its ideas.[20]

Yet even at this early stage, some special qualities of Haydn's symphonies are identified ('noble and intense, always graceful, always varied, the genius of this composer seems in effect inexhaustible');[21] and the general context of any reservations is one of increasing familiarity and acceptance of Haydn's symphonies in the repertoire:

> As an ouverture a new symphony by Hayden was performed, in which grand effects are rarer than in most others by the same author. Above all the individuality of the last movement was applauded.[22]

In the first years of Le Gros's directorship, then, the regular programming of symphonies by Haydn and Mozart was a significant feature of the *Concert spirituel*. In these years, however, Mannheim and French symphonies continued in their prominent position, and the symphonies of Sterkel enjoyed a spectacular popularity which, in numbers of performances, overshadowed the symphonies of all other composers. Within a few years this situation was to alter radically, and one of the most significant landmarks in the history of Haydn reception in Paris occurred in 1781, with the performance for the first time at the *Concert spirituel* of Haydn's Stabat Mater, his first truly popular success.

'Les deux Stabats'

In 1781 Haydn's Stabat Mater of 1767 received four performances and quickly became an established part of *Concert spirituel* repertoire. We know from Haydn's letter of 27 May 1781 to the publisher Artaria that Le Gros had corresponded with Haydn concerning the Stabat Mater and reported the success of the work at the *Concert spirituel*:

> Now something from Paris. Monsieur Le Gros, *Directeur* of the Concert Spirituel, wrote me the most flattering things about my *Stabat Mater*, which was performed there four times with the greatest applause; the gentlemen asked permission to have it engraved. They made me an offer to engrave all my future works on the most favourable terms for myself, and were most surprised that I was so singularly successful in my vocal compositions.[23]

9

The popularity of Haydn's Stabat Mater is all the more striking when one considers the local tradition into which it was so readily absorbed. The first review of Haydn's Stabat Mater explains the programming innovation of Joseph Le Gros in presenting three different settings of the Stabat Mater sequence in the April concerts of 1781:

> What particularly excited the curiosity of the amateurs of music was the happy idea, conceived by the Director of the *Concert spirituel*, of performing concurrently with the Stabat of the famous Pergolèze two motets, still unknown here, composed on the same *prose* by Signor Hayden and Père Vito, a Portuguese.[24]

It should be understood that, in the context of French music in the second half of the eighteenth century, to juxtapose any work with the Stabat Mater of Pergolesi was to invoke a standard of criticism which involved more than a mere matter of relative musical competence. Pergolesi's opera *La serva padrona* had been a *cause célèbre* in the great *Querelle des Bouffons* of the 1750s and came to represent more than an operatic style: it embodied, long after the heated debates of the 1750s, aesthetic and ideological stances which remained central to Enlightenment debates concerning music.[25] The counterpart to the status of *La serva padrona* as a touchstone of taste in the opera house was the role of Pergolesi's Stabat Mater in public concerts and in particular the *Concert spirituel*. It became an established convention of the *Concert spirituel* to perform it at least once during the Lenten season, almost always on Good Friday. At the height of the *Querelle des Bouffons* in 1753 it was performed six times at the *Concert spirituel*. In subsequent years it was absent from the repertoire only in the years 1758–62 and was performed at least once in 33 of the 38 years from 1753 to 1790 and in 28 consecutive years from 1763 to 1790.[26] In all, this work received at least 82 performances, in part or in full, at the *Concert spirituel*,[27] remaining, according to press reports, as popular with Parisian audiences in the 1780s as it was in the mid eighteenth century and representing one of the most striking instances of the overlapping of 'learned' and 'popular' taste in eighteenth-century France. To reviewers it remained a 'sublime' work which embodied the key values of French Enlightenment music aesthetics, a work which 'unites great expression and a great simplicity'.[28] For audiences, even in the 1780s, the omission of an expected performance of

Pergolesi's work was an outrage, even if the Stabat Mater of Haydn was the replacement, as the following report of 1785 makes clear:

> It is an old custom on Good Friday to perform Pergolesi's Stabat. M. le Gros was not able to conform to it this year; he was short two people to sing it: the public, which did not know or did not wish to know the cause of this impediment, or did not take account of it, showed its [bad] humour in that little reasonable way which is unhappily beginning to be introduced at this spectacle as at others. It was during Haydn's Stabat that the discontent manifested itself; the anger was vented on this work which a success of several years ought to have put beyond any displeasure. It was during one of the most beautiful pieces sung exceptionally well by M. Laïs; but just a few days before, a performance by M. Laïs of the same piece had obtained applause as universal as it was merited.[29]

During Le Gros's directorship of the *Concert spirituel* Pergolesi's Stabat Mater remained an established institution; and in his practice of performing more than one setting in a season, Le Gros enhanced the focus of attention for the Lenten season of concerts.[30] Of the three Stabat Mater settings performed in 1781, that by Père Vito was dismissed by critics and was not performed again. The performance of Haydn's setting was, on the other hand, a decided success with audiences and with the critics, who measured it in lengthy reviews by the standards of Pergolesi's setting:

> That of M. Hayden had a decided success. Its beginning is noble and touching; there is much skill and intelligence in the easy transition by which the musicians pass from the first strophe, which he has made a solo, to the second, which he has set expressively for choir. The piece 'Vidit suum dulcem natum' heralds the great resources of the composer, as does the quartet 'Virgo Virginum praeclara', interspersed from time to time with a short chorus [*petit choeur*] producing a most seductive effect. The accompaniment part is brilliant and strong: in a word, worthy of the excellent master of whom we speak.[31]

If the performance of his Stabat Mater marked the recognition of Haydn by French audiences and critics as a 'grand Maître', increasing familiarity with the work reinforced Haydn's status. It received at least one performance in each of the ten years from 1781 to 1790, being performed, in full or in part, in at least 25 concerts in this period. Perhaps more than any other single work, the Stabat Mater established Haydn's reputation with the Parisian audiences, joining Pergolesi's setting as an institution of the *Concert spirituel* – 'Les deux Stabats', to which numerous reviews refer.[32] Already in 1781 the *Mercure de France* reported that Haydn's Stabat Mater had 'found a great number of admirers; Pergolèze retained his, as well as the pure glory of having treated some strophes of his *prose* with such expression, taste and truth that if it is possible to approach it, it is at least very difficult to attain it'.[33] Subsequent reviews, for the most part, simply reaffirm the established place of Haydn's work in the repertoire,[34] while lengthier comments on Pergolesi's Stabat Mater provide the reviewers with opportunities to at once pronounce on favourite aesthetic arguments and measure the performance against long-established performance conventions and a long association of Europe's leading singers with Pergolesi's Stabat Mater at the *Concert spirituel*.[35]

When in 1783 Le Gros again introduced a third setting of the Stabat Mater into the repertoire, the new setting by Beck was found lacking in unity of expression by the established standards of the Pergolesi and Haydn settings.[36] Performances of Haydn's Stabat Mater in the same season affirmed that it was 'the only [setting] which could hold up beside that of Pergolèse'.[37] Rispoli's Stabat Mater fared somewhat better with critics and audiences than Vito's or Beck's settings when it was introduced alongside the settings of Pergolesi and Haydn in the 1786 season.[38] It was repeated in 1787 and 1788, and some reviews referred to the 'three Stabats' and to the 'accustomed success' of all three.[39] However, remaining in the repertoire for only three years, the Rispoli Stabat Mater never became the standard repertoire item that the Pergolesi and Haydn settings had become.

In programming other Stabat Mater settings with Pergolesi's, Le Gros cleverly sustained interest in an established convention of the *Concert spirituel*, and against the background of such a strong local tradition the enormous popularity of Haydn's Stabat Mater in Paris in the 1780s is particularly significant. It is also significant and, in the light of Haydn's subsequent historical reputation, somewhat surprising that it is a vocal work which first established his reputation with French audiences, and that this work should be judged successful by the criterion of French Enlightenment aesthetics – the learned taste to which I shall return. Haydn's Stabat Mater was in fact performed more frequently than Pergolesi's in the years 1777–90, yet the real testimony to its success was that it should join Pergolesi's work as one of the venerable institutions of the *Concert spirituel*.

Hegemony and genius

The success of Haydn's Stabat Mater was paralleled by, or may indeed have precipitated, the exponential increase in the number of symphonies by Haydn performed at the *Concert spirituel* in the years following the premiere of the Stabat Mater in 1781. In 1782 for the first time more Haydn than Sterkel symphonies were performed, and thereafter the spectacular but short-lived popularity of Sterkel's symphonies waned very quickly: apart from a single performance in 1783 and two in 1785, Sterkel's symphonies disappeared from the *Concert spirituel* repertoire. Mozart's relative popularity also declined, with two-thirds of the fifteen performances of his symphonies at the *Concert spirituel* occurring before 1783. At the same time Mannheim and French symphonies were eclipsed by the new dominance of Haydn. French music continued, of course, to be widely performed, and just as Gossec's vocal music was performed frequently at the *Concert spirituel* in the 1780s, other French composers dominated the enormously popular repertoire of concertos and *symphonies concertantes*. While symphonies by French composers featured in the *Concert spirituel* until 1790, they did so in ever-decreasing numbers in the 1780s and with no single composer receiving consistent performances; even Gossec's symphonies virtually disappeared from programmes after 1782. Similarly, the popularity of Mannheim symphonies was eroded in the 1780s. Symphonies by Cannabich were occasionally performed and Toeschi symphonies persisted in the repertoire, receiving one or two performances each year from 1773 to 1786. Nevertheless, in the second half of the 1780s Toeschi's symphonies also faded from the repertoire, receiving only three performances from 1785 to 1790.

The void left by the decline in popularity of the stable symphonic repertoire of the late 1770s was filled by the new and unprecedented emphasis on Haydn's symphonies (see Table 2.1). This increase is reflected in the maximum number of performances of symphonies by individual composers in a single year (Haydn 37 in 1788 and 1789, against Sterkel 12 in 1779, Gossec 8 in 1777, and Mozart 3 in 1778 and

Table 2.1. *Haydn performances at the* Concert spirituel, *1777–90*

Year	Total no. of performances	Symphonies	Stabat Mater	Others
1777	1	1		
1778	2	2		
1779	5	5		
1780	5	5		
1781	9	4	4 (in 5)	
1782	14	11	3	
1783	21	19	2	
1784	23	20	1 (in 2)	1
1785	26	20	3 (in 4)	2
1786	33	31	2	
1787	21	19	2	
1788	39	37	2	
1789	40	37	2	1
1790 (to May)	21	20	1	
Total	*260*	*231*	*25*	*4*

1779); and in the total number of symphony performances over the period 1777–90 (Haydn 231, Sterkel 50, Gossec 24, Mozart 15, Toeschi 12). The number of symphonies performed at the *Concert spirituel* increased significantly over the period in question, while at the same time there is a fairly dramatic drop in the number of composers represented, particularly in the last three years. The extent to which Haydn dominated the symphonic repertoire in the late 1780s is perhaps best seen in the number of Haydn symphonies performed, expressed as a percentage of the total number of symphonies performed, which increases from 3% in 1777 to the high point of 90% in 1788. From 1783 Haydn symphonies never make up less than 57% of the symphonies performed, and in the years 1788–90 never less than 80% (see Table 2.2).

The increasing prominence of Haydn's music in performance was paralleled by the recognition by critics of Haydn as a master of the symphonic art, the model by which other composers of symphonies were evaluated, in much the same way as Pergolesi provided a model for the judgement of vocal music. In the 1779 review quoted above, Toeschi was

Table 2.2. *Symphonies performed at the* Concert spirituel, *1777–90*

Year	No. of symphonies performed	No. of composers represented	% of symphonies by Haydn
1777	29	11+	3
1778	24	10	8
1779	26	7	19
1780	24	10	20
1781	23	13	17
1782	28	8	39
1783	26+	7+	73
1784	31	10	64.5
1785	35	13	57
1786	41	9	75
1787	30	9	63
1788	41	4	90
1789	44	5	84
1790 (to May)	25	3	80

proclaimed as the foremost symphonist, and this is consistent with the general view in Paris in the late 1770s of Toeschi, Cannabich and other second-generation Mannheim composers as inheritors of the Stamitz tradition and models of good taste in symphonic writing. By 1782 increased familiarity with Haydn's symphonies led to the admission of Haydn into the pantheon of leading symphonists. In the following extract from a review of a Haydn symphony, the current popularity of Haydn's symphonies is joined to the esteem in which the Mannheim symphonists were held, creating a Germanic-centred view of the modern symphonic repertoire.

> The symphony of Haydn with which the concert began was well performed and pleased generally. This charming composer, by the brilliance, the grace, the novelty of his ideas, has found the art of covering himself in glory and of placing himself among the first rank in a genre which the grand masters of his country, Stamitz, Toeschi, etc., seemed to have exhausted; for it must be acknowledged that it is to Germany that one is indebted for the best symphonic composers.[40]

The significance of the view of the symphony put forward here should not be underestimated: in effect, by ignoring a long and continuing tradition of French and Italian symphonies at the *Concert spirituel*, by forging a connection between Haydn and Mannheim in a significant act of historical interpretation, the current popularity of Haydn's symphonies was given a Germanic prehistory, and the hegemony of the 'symphonie allemande' was born. The hegemony of the German symphony, more often associated in the modern literature with Beethoven and the nineteenth century, is in fact established in French criticism of the 1780s and is witnessed in the critical response to the performance of symphonies by non-German composers. When in a *Concert spirituel* on 8 September 1785 a symphony and three arias by Cherubini were performed, the review is dismissive of symphonies by Italians, while the arias were somewhat better received:

> The Concert of the 8th of this month [September 1785] featured several pieces by a new Italian composer, M. Cherubini, namely, a symphony and three arias. The symphony ought to confirm our opinion that this genre is not one in which the Italian masters distinguish themselves. The arias seemed to have greater merit; however, one found that they testified to the youth of the composer, to the incoherence of ideas and to the lack of character and interest in the motifs.[41]

Within what is increasingly perceived as a Germanic-centred genre Haydn's symphonies became a new critical standard. In this regard the period 1778–89 can be seen as (in Barry Brook's term) the 'Apogée de la Symphonie [française]' only in terms of the number of French symphonies produced, since the period coincides with a sharp decline in the critical estimation of French symphonies relative to Haydn's works. When a symphony by Ragué was performed in the *Concert spirituel* of 1 November 1786, the first and third movements were described as 'well written although a little monotonous', while the second movement 'entirely in the style of M. Haydn was loudly applauded'.[42] In the following year a review of a Guénin symphony praised the composer for preserving a personal style against the very common manner of imitating the style of Haydn.

> The symphony of M. Guénin, with which the concert of the 2nd of this month began [February 1787], was heard with new pleasure. One was par-

ticularly grateful to this composer for having retained his own manner, and for refraining from the all-too-common mania for imitating the style of M. Haydn. Young people who follow this career ought to be persuaded that one always imitates badly, and that an imitator is never held in high regard. It is believed all too often today that in accumulating extraordinary modulations, in cutting up phrases, in favouring strange and even baroque melodies, one has found this style; but the style of M. Haydn is full of grace and of the choicest melody.[43]

A later review which mentions symphonies by Guénin, quoted *in extenso* below, finds it sufficient to remark that 'it is relatively high praise for them to say that they were applauded along with those of the great master [Haydn]'. Even the Mannheim style, the epitome of symphonic taste in the 1770s, is in the 1780s subjected to the same comparison with Haydn symphonies. It is interesting, for instance, to trace the declining status of Toeschi's symphonies relative to those of Haydn in the 1780s. In the 1779 review quoted above, Toeschi was regarded as set apart from other symphony composers, and in the review of 16 November 1782 Toeschi, together with Stamitz etc., were the models adduced to affirm Haydn's acceptance as a 'grand Maître', 'among the first rank' of German symphonists. By 1783, however, the praise given a performance of a Toeschi symphony is tempered by an unfavourable comparison with Haydn's symphonies:

> We do not know if the symphony of M. Toëschi, with which the concert of the 8th of this month [September 1783] began, is newly composed, but it has not been heard here before. It had a beautiful effect; one does not perhaps find there the same brilliant gestures [*tournures brillantes*] of M. Hayden; but it has, like all the works of this grand master, a vigorous harmony, and a sturdy manner which also has merit.[44]

Toeschi's solidly constructed and worthy symphonies earned him the respect of a *grand maître*, and other composers, even measured against Haydn's symphonies, may have earned a certain degree of approval, but all lacked, according to criticism of the 1780s, a quality which elevated Haydn's works above the works of others, be they successful, popular, or merely competent, and this quality was, especially in the second half of the 1780s, identified, either explicitly or implicitly, as the quality of genius.

The notion of genius is central to the contemporary understanding of creativity and, as such, is a prominent idea in literature, philosophy, and aesthetics. Genius was variously defined, but generally in eighteenth-century thought it was understood as an innate quality in the individual, bestowed by nature. As formulated, influentially, by Immanuel Kant, it is, in many ways, closer in type to the Romantic genius of the nineteenth century than to earlier notions of divinely inspired genius; and it has as its primary characteristic the capacity for originality. Although, according to Kant, 'every art presupposes rules, which serve as the foundation', genius 'is the talent (natural endowment) which gives the rule to art': it is 'a *talent* for producing something for which no determinate rule can be given, and not a predisposition consisting of a skill for something that can be learned by following some rule or other; hence the foremost property of genius must be *originality*'. Genius in Enlightenment thought is also exemplary; its 'products ... must also be models' which must serve 'as a standard or rule by which to judge'; and it is a gift of nature by which the author is enabled to produce a work of genius although 'he himself does not know how he came by the ideas for it', nor can he 'communicate [his procedure] to others in precepts that would enable them to bring about like products'.[45]

Enlightenment concepts of genius are never systematically articulated in connection with Haydn's music in French criticism of the 1780s, but the characteristics increasingly attributed to it mirror the language of such general concepts. The word 'genius' itself, which is not employed lightly or loosely in the eighteenth century, is frequently used in reviews of the later 1780s to distinguish the quality of originality found in Haydn's symphonies from those of others. In many reviews, including those quoted above, the comparisons and assertions concerning imitators of Haydn's style are not in themselves of any great importance, nor are they, from today's perspective, necessarily supportable stylistically; what is significant, however, is that the reviewers, in insisting on the exemplary quality of Haydn's symphonies, are attributing to Haydn a characteristic of genius. In terms of eighteenth-century thinking, it follows that his symphonies, as the products of genius, may be considered 'fine art', which is, according to Kant, 'possible only as the product of genius'.[46]

In the context of eighteenth-century concepts of genius, the assessment of the Pleyel symphonies performed in the *Concert spirituel* in March 1787 is revealing:

> The novelties which one heard in the last two concerts were two sym-
> phonies of M. Pleyel, a pupil of M. Haydn. They were warmly applauded.
> If M. Pleyel has not the original genius of his master, because genius does
> not transmit itself, he owes at least to his lessons a firm and sure touch and
> a great knowledge of the effects of harmony.[47]

In this and numerous other reviews, the extent to which the genius of
Haydn had come to dominate the reception of symphonies in Paris is
abundantly clear. Pleyel's mere competence is contrasted with the
originality and genius attributed to Haydn. It is also clear that Haydn's
works are regarded as exemplary (self-evidently, the 'standard or rule' by
which the reviewer judges Pleyel's work), and it is implicit that the
elusive quality of genius is a gift of nature since genius is not transmitted.

While in reviews from the later 1780s the recognition of Haydn as a
genius in these terms emerges piecemeal, writings about Haydn in the
late eighteenth and early nineteenth centuries, including the German
criticism of Reichardt and others and the earliest Haydn biographies, are
increasingly informed by such concepts. In a well-known passage from
Griesinger's contemporary biography of Haydn, for instance, Haydn's
view of creativity – his 'theoretical *raisonnements*', as reported by
Griesinger – is formulated in a way that has much in common with the
writings of Kant and others on the notion of genius.

> His [Haydn's] theoretical *raisonnements* were very simple: namely, a piece
> of music ought to have a fluent melody, coherent ideas, no superfluous
> ornaments, nothing overdone, no confusing accompaniment, and so
> forth. How to satisfy these requirements? That, he confessed himself,
> cannot be learned by rules, and simply depends on natural talent and on
> the inspiration of inborn genius.
>
> Someone told Haydn that Albrechtsberger wished to see all fourths
> banished from the purest style. 'What does that mean?' replied Haydn.
> 'Art is free, and will be limited by no pedestrian rules. The ear, assuming
> that it is trained, must decide, and I consider myself as competent as any to
> legislate here. Such affectations are worthless. I would rather someone
> tried to compose a really *new* minuet.'
>
> Haydn always composed his works at the clavier. 'I sat down, began to
> improvise, sad or happy according to my mood, serious or trifling. Once I
> had seized upon an idea, my whole endeavor was to develop and sustain it
> in keeping with the rules of the art. Thus I sought to keep going, and this is
> where so many of our new composers fall down. They string out one little

piece after another, they break off when they have hardly begun, and nothing remains in the heart when one has listened to it.'

He also took exception to the fact that so many musicians now composed who had never learned how to sing. 'Singing must almost be counted among the lost arts, and instead of song they let instruments dominate.'[48]

There are many points of interest in this passage, and I will return to it in another connection; but for present purposes the views on the relationship between rules and originality and the source of Haydn's originality are worth emphasising. That, in Kant's words, 'every art presupposes rules which serve as the foundation [of art]' is acknowledged in Haydn's aim in composing 'to develop and sustain it [an idea] in keeping with the rules of art'; at the same time Haydn's opinion on Albrechtsberger's rules for strict composition, his assertion that 'art is free, and will be limited by no pedestrian rules', and his placement of the challenge of writing 'a really *new* minuet' ahead of mere correctness all closely echo the Kantian precepts that originality is the 'foremost property' of genius and that genius alone 'gives the rule to art'. Similarly, the belief that genius is a 'natural endowment' which cannot be explained scientifically or methodically, or communicated to another, is mirrored in the admission that Haydn's compositional objectives 'cannot be learned by rules' but depend entirely 'on natural talent and the inspiration of inborn genius'.

The apogee of the Haydn symphony at the *Concert spirituel*, 1788–90

In the years 1788 to 1790 the ascendancy of the Haydn symphony at the *Concert spirituel* was complete, and the number of performances of symphonies by other composers is statistically negligible. Only eight composers, apart from Haydn, are represented (three in 1788, four in 1789, and two in 1790), of whom five received only a single performance of a symphony (see Table 2.3). It is noticeable that within this Haydn-dominated programming, French symphonies maintain a continued, albeit much reduced, presence, but that Mannheim symphonies have virtually disappeared from the repertoire, being represented by a single performance of a Toeschi symphony.

Table 2.3. *Symphonies performed at the*
Concert spirituel, *1788–90*

Composer	No. of performances (%)
Haydn	94 (85.5%)
Lachnitz	7 (6.3%)
Guénin	2 (1.8%)
Pleyel	2 (1.8%)
Rigel fils	1 (0.9%)
Mozart	1 (0.9%)
Toeschi	1 (0.9%)
Candeille	1 (0.9%)
'un amateur célèbre'	1 (0.9%)

The numerical dominance of Haydn's symphonies is all the more striking in a context in which the overall number of symphonies performed per year is significantly higher than in the early years of Le Gros's directorship of the *Concert spirituel* (see Table 2.2). It is apparent that the increased importance of the symphony as a genre is inextricably linked to the popularity of Haydn symphonies and to a programming innovation by Le Gros, whereby rather than one symphony serving as an overture to the whole concert, as in the earlier years of the *Concert spirituel*, two symphonies were heard in most concerts in the late 1780s, usually with one beginning each half of the concert.[49] When in 1779 Le Gros used symphonies by Sterkel and Mozart to begin each half of a concert, the *Mercure de France* remarked on this innovation.[50] From 1788 to 1790 this format was increasingly a standard practice, and it is common that each of the two symphonies in this new format was by Haydn. In these three years Haydn compositions were performed in all but two of the 62 *Concerts spirituels* given, and in more than half of the concerts two Haydn compositions were featured.[51]

Although it is not possible to write directly about the reception of Haydn's 'Paris' Symphonies, it is probable that the high point in the success of Haydn's symphonies at the *Concert spirituel* in 1788–90 is directly connected with performances of these works. Symphonies Nos. 82–7 were of course first introduced to the French public in the *Concert de la Loge Olympique*, probably sometime in 1787. The advertisement for the Imbault edition of these works which appeared in January 1788 specifically identified them with this concert series:

> From the Repertoire of the *Loge Olympique*
>
> six symphonies for diverse instruments; composed by J. Haydn, Œuv. 51e., engraved after the original scores belonging to the *Loge Olympique*. Price, 15 liv.; each of the symphonies is for sale separately at 3 liv. In Paris, chez Imbault, rue S. Honoré, between the Hôtel d'Aligre & rue de Poulies, N⁰ 627.
>
> These symphonies, of the most beautiful character and astonishing construction, cannot but be sought out with the greatest eagerness by those who have the good fortune to hear them, and even by those who do not know them. The name of Haydn vouches for their extraordinary merit.[52]

These latest of Haydn's symphonies were therefore known at least by repute to a wide audience by January 1788, and in the course of 1788 numerous advertisements appeared in the *Mercure de France* for arrangements of the symphonies for string quartet, keyboard trio, etc.[53] It is also in 1788 that a much-quoted review, commonly associated with the 'Paris' Symphonies, appeared in the *Mercure de France*:

> Symphonies by M. Haydn were performed at practically all the concerts. Each day one is more aware of, and consequently one admires more, the work of this great genius, who, in each of his pieces, knows so well how to draw such rich and varied developments from a single subject [*sujet unique*]; so unlike those sterile composers who continuously move from one idea to another for lack of knowing how to present one [idea] in varied forms, and mechanically pile up effect on effect, without connection and without taste. The symphonies of M. Haydn, always sure in their effect, would produce even greater effect if the room were more resonant, and if its narrow shape had allowed the director of this concert to arrange the orchestra more advantageously. Some symphonies by M. Guénin were also performed, and it is relatively high praise for them to say that they were applauded along with those of the great master.[54]

Robbins Landon has suggested that this review 'appears to refer' to the 'Paris' Symphonies 'when they were played at the 1787 season of the *Concert Spirituel*'.[55] However, Landon's unexplained editorial interpolation '[l'année dernière]' into the first sentence quoted above ('On a exécuté à tous les Concerts[56] [l'année dernière] des Symphonies de M. Haydn') is misleading, and the assertion that the 'Paris' Symphonies were performed at the *Concert spirituel* in 1787, repeated subsequently by other authors,[57] is without foundation. It seems to me quite likely that this review refers to at least some of the 'Paris' Symphonies, but that the performances at the *Concert spirituel* occurred in 1788. The beginning of this report clearly refers to the concerts of 'cette quinzaine'.[58] There were no concerts in April 1788, but from the works and composers mentioned, other than Haydn symphonies, it would appear that the review refers to all the concerts given in March 1788, that is, fifteen concerts between 9 and 31 March.[59] The dating of the performances of Haydn symphonies mentioned in the review is supported by a number of other factors. First, while the Imbault print advertised in January 1788 refers to these works as 'Du Répertoire de la Loge Olympique', some editions which appeared later in 1788 have the legend 'exécuté à la Loge Olympique et au Concert Spirituel'.[60] We know from this that at least some of the 'Paris' Symphonies were performed at the *Concert spirituel* before the end of 1788. Secondly, it seems to me likely that in 1787 the *Concerts spirituels* were largely reliant on repeat performances of popular older Haydn symphonies, and few 'new' symphonies (in the sense of symphonies performed for the first time at the *Concert spirituel*) were apparently given in that year. Indeed, in the rapid increase in the number of Haydn symphonies performed at the *Concert spirituel* in the 1780s, the year 1787 represents a minor anomaly in the trend of ever-increasing performances of Haydn symphonies (see Table 2.1). On the other hand, in 1788 the trend of the previous years is accelerated, and a large number of the symphonies performed are identified in concert advertisements as 'new' symphonies. In the concerts of March 1788 twenty Haydn symphonies were performed, and in various sources at least five of them are identified as 'new'.

The high point in the number of Haydn performances at the *Concert spirituel* reached in the years 1788–90 is compatible with the availability, after the initial performances at the *Loge Olympique*, of a new batch of Haydn symphonies. If 1788 seems the most likely date for the introduction of Symphonies Nos. 82–7 into the *Concert spirituel* repertoire, no doubt they were repeated in subsequent years.[61] It is also likely that Symphonies Nos. 88–92 (the 'Tost' Symphonies, Nos. 88–9, and the second set written for the Comte d'Ogny, Nos. 90–2) found their way into the *Concert spirituel* repertoire in 1789 and 1790; it is certainly the case that at least one of the symphonies written for Tost (No. 89) was performed at the *Concert spirituel* in 1790 (on 31 March and 5 April), since it was identified as 'no. 29', which corresponds to its publication as no. 29 of Sieber's *Symphonies périodiques*.[62]

The extent to which Parisian audiences were exposed to Haydn's works in the years 1788–90 amounts to a virtual prolonged *Haydnfest*. The performance of the 'Paris' Symphonies at the *Concert spirituel* represents the climax of a trend of increasing popularity of Haydn's works which spans the 1780s, and the eulogy to Haydn's symphonies in the *Mercure de France* on 12 April 1788 reinforces the critical estimation of Haydn which had emerged in the Parisian press particularly since 1782. It mentions the ubiquity of Haydn's music at the *Concert spirituel*, the perceived superiority of Haydn's symphonies over those of his contemporaries, and the status of Haydn as a *grand Maître*, a genius, the standard by which other composers of symphonies (in this case Guénin) are measured. The success of Haydn's music in Paris is therefore no less extensive or significant than the composer's more copiously documented triumphs during his sojourns in London in the 1790s.[63] Indeed, the particular affinity of Parisian audiences with Haydn's music which developed in the 1780s was not to be short-lived: well into the second decade of the nineteenth century Haydn's symphonies remained the most performed and most esteemed symphonies in Paris concerts, decidedly overshadowing the symphonies of Mozart and even the early symphonies of Beethoven,[64] and Haydn's status as a symphonist in the late eighteenth century remained, apparently, relevant as late as 1820:

> Haydn, in carrying the grand symphony to a point of perfection, which it seems impossible to surpass, had at the same time raised his own glory, and that of his nation to the highest pitch.[65]

The verdicts of the eighteenth century, stated, as they often are, as apparently naive assertions concerning the inherent virtues of a composer, do not, of course, necessarily conform to views expressed with the arrogance of hindsight and with the aid of the elaborate methodologies of modern analysis and criticism. It is difficult by today's standards to justify the popularity of Sterkel's symphonies in the late 1770s and early

1780s by comparison with the relative neglect of Mozart's instrumental music in Paris. Eighteenth-century concert reports on the symphonic repertoire are not of any great value as music criticism, yet they raise pressing questions concerning the basis of contemporary judgements, which, however alien to modern aesthetics, are inevitably a part of the history of eighteenth-century music. A search for the aesthetic basis for the apparent Haydnmania described in the preceding pages is the subject of following chapters.

3

Popular taste

The focus on the symphonic repertoire of the *Concert spirituel* serves to illustrate some important aspects of the reception of Haydn's music in Paris. Yet in the public perception of the eighteenth century other genres of instrumental music had, for most of the century, a higher profile.[1] Central to the popularity and importance of the *Concert spirituel* was a veritable cult of virtuosity associated with the concerto and the *symphonie concertante*, a crucial facet of French musical taste which indirectly contributes to an understanding of the French appreciation of Haydn's music. In the second half of the eighteenth century especially, the *Concert spirituel*, while preserving some venerable French musical traditions, was increasingly international in both repertoire and personnel, and its international reputation as a concert series rested in no small part on the fact that it was one of the most prestigious venues for the talents of Europe's foremost instrumental virtuosos. A performance at the *Concert spirituel* in 1786 by the clarinettist Michel Yost, commonly known as Monsieur Michel,[2] justified, according to one reviewer, the commonly held view that Paris was the leading European centre for the performance of instrumental music:

> M. Michel . . . seems to have brought the clarinet to the highest point of perfection, [and] to have proved that in instrumental music we do not yield to any European city; for we must count among our musical riches the foreign artists who have settled amongst us. It would be difficult to assemble elsewhere greater talent than one could in Paris, and it counts for much that the *Concert* [*spirituel*] should have assembled them all.[3]

Much of the attraction of the *Concert spirituel* rested on its variety, with a typical eighteenth-century blend of vocal items (arias, motets, oratorios etc.), symphonies, and vehicles for the display of instrumental virtuosos, mainly concertos and *symphonies concertantes*. The following programme for a *Concert spirituel* on 16 April 1786 illustrates some typical features in the format of concerts in the mid 1780s:

> Concert Spirituel Auj[our d'hui]. 16, à 6 h ½. Ire Partie: Symph. de M. Hayden, après laquelle Melle Vaillant chantera un Air It[alien]. M. Michel exécutera un Concerto de clarinette, de sa comp[osition]. M. David chantera un Air It[alien]. 2de Partie: Symph[onie] concertante à 2 violons de M. Bertheaume, qui exécutera avec M. Grasset. Ensuite, M. Rousseau chantera une Scène Franç[aise] paroles de M. Moline, musique de M. Berton. M. Duport exécutera un Concerto de violoncelle., de sa comp[osition]. M. David chantera un Air It[alien].[4]

Although, as mentioned above, the inclusion of two symphonies, frequently both by Haydn, was increasingly common in the *Concert spirituel* of the later 1780s, and although some concerts each year contained a higher proportion of vocal music, this programme is typical in featuring three works for soloists and orchestra (two concertos and a *symphonie concertante*). In the period of Le Gros's directorship Mannheim musicians continued, as composers and soloists, to exert a strong influence on programming;[5] in the 1782 and 1783 seasons, when Haydn's Stabat Mater was becoming a Parisian institution, Viotti was also a star attraction; and the galaxy of international celebrities supplemented the large number of native French virtuosos (Devienne (flute), Lebrun (horn), Michel (clarinet), Ozi (bassoon), Duport and Bréval (cello), and many others) who were regular performers at the *Concert spirituel* and enjoyed the enthusiastic following, not infrequently tinged with a nationalistic bias.

By the 1780s almost every orchestral instrument was represented in the concerto repertoire of the *Concert spirituel*,[6] the clarinet concerto had been popularised, and performances of concertos for the fortepiano were more frequent.[7] However, the most conspicuous manifestation of the Parisian popular taste for instrumental virtuosity and of the diversity of the repertoire for soloists and orchestra is represented in the flourishing of the *symphonie concertante* from the 1770s. These frequently lightweight compositions, often in two movements, featured, two, three, four or more soloists, and the diversity of solo intrumental combinations was immense. The vast output of *symphonies concertantes* is associated in particular with French composers, who, according to Barry Brook, produced more than twice the number of *symphonies concertantes* as the rest of Europe together, the bulk of this (113 from a total of 242 works, according to Brook's figures) in the period 1778–89.[8] In these years the high point in the production of French *symphonies concertantes* is matched by a decline in the production of French symphonies,[9] and it is very probably true that at least some French composers increasingly concentrated on the *symphonie concertante* in the light of the growing dominance of the symphonic repertoire by Haydn's works.

Thus, in the *Concert spirituel* of the 1780s there is, alongside a diverse solo concerto repertoire, a burgeoning of an even more diverse repertoire of concertos for multiple soloists. The seemingly inexhaustible Parisian popular taste for instrumental virtuosity and colourful display which these repertoires represent is contemporaneous with, and seemingly in no way diminished by, the increase in the prestige of the symphony in the 1780s; on the contrary, it is possible to argue that the appeal of the popular taste for instrumental virtuosity was a prerequisite for a popular success in all public instrumental genres, including the symphony.

The notion of 'popular taste' is itself complex and not without contradictions, some of which will be discussed below, but it seems clear that there was a general enthusiasm among Parisian audiences for a virtuoso repertoire which is reflected in the high percentage of concertos and *symphonies concertantes* in the *Concert spirituel* programmes. Notwithstanding the mixture of viewpoints, the various hidden agendas and the ideological biases presented in the Parisian press of the 1780s, it is also true that the concert reports of the 1780s reflect, to an extent, contemporary popular musical taste. The apparent aim of the concert reports in the *Mercure de France* was not to 'recount the sensations of the moment' but rather to 'report . . . public opinions after they are fixed',[10] and while it would be naive to assume that this was done without prejudice, nevertheless there is a transparent aspect to most concert reports. Large sections of such reports are concerned with direct reporting of the works performed, the performers involved, the novelties (in the sense of those works and performers heard for the first time) and the audience reaction. There is little reason to doubt the repeated reports of the success of a work or a performer, especially when this popularity can be confirmed by the concert programmes and sometimes by other independent testimony.

While the reports of the Parisian press confirm that the virtuoso tradition was an important aspect of popular taste, there is also a strand of thought in many of these reports which presents professional opinion, the judgement of the *savant*.[11] Sections of many reports comment in technical detail on the merits of a performance or compare the relative merits of two of more performers. Ensemble, intonation, the layout of the orchestra, the quality of sound, the vocal qualities of individual singers, and other technical matters are mentioned in many reviews in a way that is not dissimilar to modern concert reviewing. The virtuoso tradition of the *Concert spirituel* can therefore be said to be of central concern both to a largely amateur popular taste and to the professional taste of the *savant*, and the successful composer and performer within this tradition might aim to earn both the adulation of the audience and the admiration of the *savant*.

The virtuoso repertoire of the concerto and the *symphonie concertante* is not one with which Haydn is obviously or strongly associated, either from the perspective of eighteenth-century audiences or from that of the modern scholarly literature. His only *symphonie concertante* (Hob. I:105) was written in 1792 during his first London visit, and at the *Concert spirituel* Haydn concertos were rarely played.[12] However, the appeal of Haydn's symphonies to French audiences is not unconnected to the cult of virtuosity of the *Concert spirituel*, and Haydn's most frequently performed symphonies in the period 1784 to 1787 indicate the proximity of Haydn's symphonies to the French virtuoso tradition.

Jean Lebrun (1759–1809), a noted horn player, ubiquitous in the *Concert spirituel* of the 1780s, featured as a soloist in horn concertos and in numerous *symphonies concertantes* of his own composition and by others. He was also a horn player in the Orchestre de la Société Olympique in 1786, quite possibly playing in the first performance of Haydn's 'Paris' Symphonies.[13] Interestingly, he was also acclaimed in Paris for his solos in performances of symphonies. A review of a Vogel symphony performed on 2 February 1784 specifically mentions that 'the horn solos of the second piece were performed perfectly by M. Lebrun'.[14] This was not, apparently, an isolated event, and the closeness of the virtuoso tradition to the symphonic genre is emphasised in a further observation concerning Lebrun's performance of the solo horn part in a *symphonie concertante* by Devienne:

> M. Lebrun, playing the horn part, despite the great success he had already had in several Haydn symphonies, far surpassed the favourable opinion one had already formed of his talents.[15]

The 'plusieurs symphonies d'Haydn' in which Lebrun played solos most probably refers to performances advertised as 'Symphonie de M. Haydn, hautbois & cors obligés' or '[avec] hautbois & cors récitans'.[16] Seven performances of Haydn symphonies between 8 December 1784 and 9 December 1790 were so advertised, and a further symphony was advertised as having horn obbligatos.[17] It is not possible to identify these Haydn symphonies, but there are a number of Haydn works which would certainly have provided suitable vehicles for Lebrun's talents and could be described as having parts for 'hautbois & cors obligés'. Symphony No. 73 ('La Chasse'), with its virtuoso horn solos in the finale, is perhaps an obvious candidate, given the fact that it was available in Paris in 1784.[18] This symphony seems in any case to have been popular in Paris in the 1780s, and an arrangement of the work for 'Clavecin, avec violons & basse à volonté, [arrangés] par M. Wenck' was advertised in the *Mercure de France* of 4 March 1786. If it was the symphony, or one of the symphonies, associated with Lebrun's horn solos, then it follows a long tradition at the *Concert spirituel* of popular 'hunting' symphonies with such solos, by Stamitz, Gossec, and others.[19]

The virtuoso playing of Lebrun is also associated with other symphonies which were presented to the French public, in advertisements, in performances, and in some instances in publications of the music, as *symphonies concertantes* by Haydn. For the *Concert spirituel* of 7 April 1787 a work by Haydn was advertised as 'Symphonie concertante de M. Hayden, violon, violoncelle, flûte, hautbois, & cors de chasse obligés', and in one source the soloists are listed as Bertheaume (violin), Duport (cello), Duverger (flute), André (oboe) and Lebrun (horn).[20] In the years 1786–7, at a time when the *symphonie concertante* was flourishing at the *Concert spirituel*, five performances of a work or works by Haydn described as 'Symphonie concertante' were given, and four of these performances occurred in April 1786. Again it is not possible to establish definitely the identity of the work, nor is it immediately apparent whether the performances were of one or more works. In the case of four of the performances (7, 13, 22 April 1786 and 8 April 1787), the advertised descriptions suggest that the same work was performed four times: the listings of the concertante parts are consistent except for some discrepancy regarding whether there were one or more flutes and one or more horns. For the concert of 11 April 1786, however, an obbligato double-bass part is listed in addition to the concertante instruments mentioned for the other performances, and in one advertisement this work is referred to as a 'Nouvelle Symphonie concertante', distinguishing it from the Haydn *symphonie concertante* previously heard on 7 April.[21] That two different works were performed on these occasions is also suggested by a brief reference to two *symphonies concertantes* by Haydn in a 'Résumé des Concerts de Pâques' which undoubtedly refers to the concerts of the 11 and 13 April: 'Two *symphonies concertantes* by M. Hayden were performed; only one seemed worthy of the *grand Maître*'.[22] One of these works, perhaps the one less worthy of Haydn, may very well have been the symphony listed by Hoboken as Hob. I:D13, a work of dubious authenticity, but one whose publication in Paris in 1788 under Haydn's name was, significantly, advertised as a 'Simphonie concertante à 8 Instrumens obligés, 2 violons, flûte, Alto, violoncelle, basse, et 2 cors; par J. Haydn'.[23] The other work performed at these concerts was very probably also a symphony, and while a number of Haydn symphonies would easily lend themselves to adaptation for performance as *symphonies concertantes*, with the concertante parts as listed in advertisements, Symphony No. 31 ('Hornsignal') comes closest to fitting the profile, since it is rich in obbligato writing and was, moreover, published by Sieber in Paris *c*.1785 – significantly, under the title *Symphonie concertante*.

Whether 'La Chasse' and the 'Hornsignal' or other symphonies were performed on these occasions, the significant point is that the richness of the concertante writing in Haydn symphonies was appreciated in Paris and was compatible with the French taste for virtuoso concertos and *symphonies concertantes*. At least one Haydn symphony was absorbed into the Parisian *symphonie concertante* tradition,[24] and one or more symphonies with horn and oboe obbligatos form a middle ground between the symphony and the *symphonie concertante* or concerto traditions.

While the concertante writing of Haydn's symphonies illustrates most tangibly the connection between Haydn reception and popular taste, equally strong in French symphonic taste was the appreciation of splendour in orchestral writing, the expectation of powerful *tutti* writing, dramatic contrasts and grand orchestral gestures, which was to a large extent due to the influence of Mannheim symphonies in the formation of French symphonic taste.[25] As his letters make clear, Mozart recognised the importance of standard orchestral effects in symphonies placed before the French public and wrote his 'Paris' Symphony calculating the audience reaction to dramatic orchestral effects, such as surprise openings and suddenly introduced *forte tutti* sections:

> just in the middle of the first Allegro there was a passage which I felt sure must please. The audience was quite carried away – and there was a tremendous burst of applause. But as I knew, when I wrote it, what effect it would surely produce, I had introduced the passage again at the close – when there were shouts of 'Da Capo'. The Andante also found favour, but particularly the last Allegro, because, having observed that all last as well as first Allegros begin here with all the instruments playing together and generally unisono, I began mine with two violins only, piano for the first eight bars – followed instantly by a forte; the audience, as I expected, said 'hush' at the soft beginning, and when they heard the forte, began at once to clap their hands.[26]

The taste of the French *savant* was equally concerned with splendour in orchestral sonority, as witnessed in the innumerable discussions regarding orchestral sizes and the most advantageous layout of the orchestra, and the vocabulary of symphony reviews gives the impression that orchestral splendour is an important criterion for evaluation: a successful 'symphonie à grand orchestre' is repeatedly described as 'majestueuse', has a 'grand caractère', and is characterised by 'les grands effets' and 'les tournures brillantes'. In the comments reported above, for instance, a Haydn symphony disappoints one reviewer because 'the grand effects are rarer than in most other [symphonies] by the same composer'; when a Toeschi symphony is unfavourably compared with Haydn's symphonies in a 1783 review, the reason given is that 'one does not perhaps find there the same brilliant gestures of M. Haydn'. The review in the *Mercure de France* of 1788, which possibly refers to the 'Paris' Symphonies, is also relevant in this regard: the comment that Haydn symphonies are 'always sure of their effect' must be understood in terms of sonority and orchestral brilliance, since their effect would be enhanced 'if the room were more resonant, and if its narrow shape had allowed the director of this concert to arrange the orchestra more advantageously'.

The orchestral grandeur which Parisian popular taste appears to demand might have been associated in particular with Haydn's C major symphonies – a distinctive sub-genre of 'festive' symphony, customarily with elaborate brass and timpani parts – which appear to have been particularly popular in Paris and examples of which are to be found in the 'Paris' Symphonies and in a later set written for the Comte d'Ogny (Nos. 82 and 90).[27] Yet the concertante writing in symphonies presented as *symphonies concertantes* and the orchestral splendour of a C major symphony exemplify general characteristics of Haydn's symphonies which do not come into these categories. Haydn's 'Paris' Symphonies were written for an imagined international audience rather than for local performances at Eszterháza. Although he lacked first-hand experience of Parisian audiences, his musical taste was international, and it is clear that the success of the 'Paris' Symphonies built on an established perception of Haydn's symphonies as generally being compatible with Parisian popular taste.

4

Learned taste

> While waiting for dinner, Pococurante had a concerto performed.
> Candide found the music enchanting.
>   'This noise', said Pococurante, 'can give half an hour's amusement; but
> if it lasts any longer it bores everyone, though no one dares to admit it.
> Music to-day is nothing more than the art of performing difficult pieces,
> and what is merely difficult gives no lasting pleasure.[1]

Notwithstanding the idea of popular taste presented in Chapter 3, virtuosity, and indeed instrumental music in general, was frequently viewed with suspicion in the learned Enlightenment discourse on art. The view expressed by Pococurante in Voltaire's *Candide* is a typical stance whereby it is allowed that the concerto may give passing amusement, may entertain and may fulfil a social function, but it lacks the imprimatur of learned taste. Similarly, in Batteux's reduction of all fine art to a single principle, the influential Neo-Classical theory of *mimesis*, the role of instrumental music is strictly circumscribed, having only a 'half life' and being largely dependent on external factors for the clarification of its expressive meaning.[2] Although the place of music in Kant's aesthetic is problematic, he, like many writers, distinguished between art which entertains and that which has a higher aesthetic value. For Kant, 'agreeable arts are those whose purpose is merely enjoyment', and a distinction is maintained between the merely pleasurable and the disinterestedness of fine arts: 'aesthetic art that is also fine art is one whose standard is the reflective power of judgement, rather than sensation proper'.[3] Instrumental music lacked a compelling aesthetic justification in the eighteenth century, and virtuosity in instrumental music was doubly damned, anathema to aesthetic theory, which was largely tied to language models and the antithesis of 'beautiful simplicity', the aesthetic ideal of opera reform and of many of the most influential French *philosophes* who wrote about music.[4]

In the aesthetic of Rousseau sensibility is celebrated. The *raison d'être* of music is to give 'a pleasure of interest and feeling that speaks to the heart',[5] and it is through the medium of melody that music has expressive power:

> By imitating the inflections of the voice, melody expresses laments, cries of sorrow or of joy, threats, moans; all the vocal signs of passion are within its jurisdiction. It imitates the accents of languages and the turns of phrase allotted in each idiom to certain emotions of the soul. Melody does not merely imitate, it speaks; and its inarticulate but lively, ardent, passionate language has a hundred times more energy than speech itself. This is the source of the power of musical imitation; this is how melody holds sway over sensitive hearts.[6]

The authority for this view was nature itself, which, with the secularisation of thought in the eighteenth century, became the special preoccupation of the Enlightenment: it was the subject of scientific investigation, and critiques of society, law, religion and education all claimed the moral authority of nature, a secular god.[7] In the arts, nature was celebrated in the vogue for splendid gardens, and in pastoral landscapes and poetry;[8] in music, nature was reflected in a learned taste in which the aesthetic orientation towards vocal music and simplicity is explicit, as in Rousseau's article on the term 'Naturel':

> In music this word has several meanings: (i) natural music is vocal music, whilst artificial music is performed on instruments; (ii) a song is said to be natural when it is effortless, sweet, graceful, and uncomplicated; a harmony is natural when it contains few inversions and few dissonances, and when it is the product of the essential and natural chords of the mode; (iii) all melodies that are neither contrived nor baroque are said to be natural, too.[9]

The complexities of the great Enlightenment music debates are not my concern here,[10] but it is relevant that the association which Rousseau and others made between nature, the primacy of vocal music, and a simple melodic style remained current in later eighteenth-century debates on the aesthetics of music. Notwithstanding fundamental ideological differences with Rousseau,[11] Gluck's aims in his reform operas were in some important regards compatible with Rousseau: his 'greatest task [was] to seek the beauty of simplicity',[12] and his objective was to 'search for a noble, sensitive and natural melody'.[13] In the late 1770s Guy de Chabanon emphatically rejected the validity of mimetic theory in music. He was also more receptive to the aesthetic merits of instrumental music and, redressing Rousseau's exclusive concern with melody, sought to 'reconstitute the art [of music] in its entirety, by restoring to it one of its most essential accessories, harmony'. He none the less concluded that melody 'reigns supreme in music':

> Harmony is tributary and subject to melody. It should not dare anything without the consent of its sovereign. Let this truth be the first and the last of those we must establish.[14]

Given such preoccupations, the new complexity of the symphony in the 1780s and the virtuosity of concertos were problematic from the perspective of aesthetic theory. In the Parisian press of the 1780s, alongside the enthusiasm for virtuosity and splendour and the specifically musical criticism of the *savant*, one also encounters the learned aesthetic opinion of the connoisseur.[15] Reviews which proclaim the popular success of this or that symphony, concerto or soloist are intermingled with reviews which insist on the values of simplicity and noble melody, lament the decadence of virtuosos and either assert *a priori* claims for the supremacy of vocal music or ask that instrumental music conform to the aesthetic standards of vocal music. For instance, in the following extract from a 1779 review the influence of learned taste is pronounced in the reaction to concertos for violin, harp, clarinet and cello, while in other contemporary reviews the soloists mentioned are acclaimed for their technical skill and their popular appeal is acknowledged:

> The hunting-horn concerto performed on Thursday by M. Leopoldo-Colle, that for violin by M. Le Févre, [and] that for harp by M. Krumpholtz would seem to have been made less to move than to astonish the small number of connoisseurs. The three concertos performed on the following day, with M. Baer on clarinet, M. Capron on violin, and M. Duport on cello, excel in the same way; one must none the less make exception for MM. Duport and Krumpholtz, whose compositions, although learned and replete with difficult passages, still maintained an appreciable melody, and pleased the untrained ears as well as those of the *savant*.

The director of this concert, M. le Gros, who looks for every possible means to make each day more interesting, must undoubtedly worry about not being able to persuade the majority of the virtuosos to follow his example, that is to say, to imitate the beautiful simplicity of his singing in their instrumental music. Are not simplicity and the natural, then, the complement to perfection, the distinctive character of masterpieces in every genre? Is there not a middle way between the Pont-neuf airs and the bravura pieces in which the public grasps hold neither of the details nor of the whole?[16]

Here the poetics of simplicity, sensibility and melody to a large degree predetermine the critical response to the concertos performed. The objections to the embellishments of virtuosos are conventional in the literature, similar in kind to Gluck's objections to cadenzas and the embellishment of da capo repeats in arias and to numerous other reviews of instrumental music. The art of the virtuoso is, almost by definition, capable only of astonishing an audience, without, as is stated elsewhere in this review, 'penetrating the seat of the passions'. The reviewer demands nothing less than that virtuosos deny their very nature in the service of a universal principle, 'simplicity and the natural', which 'is the distinctive character of masterpieces in every genre'. It is a fair assumption that the middle way between street songs and bravura pieces which the review advocates for the future of the concerto is roughly akin to the beautiful simplicity of opera aesthetics.

This review is concerned with a critique of the concerto and the virtuoso by the aesthetic standards of vocal music, but all instrumental genres were subject to the same type of scrutiny. In instrumental music of the second half of the eighteenth century the compositional commonplace which is most obviously problematic for contemporary aesthetic theory is contrast. It is therefore no surprise that the more dynamic affective genius of instrumental music, by comparison with an aria, for instance, should appear to some reviewers as confusion: one is presented with 'eternal variations without variety', with 'twenty disparate subjects', with 'twenty modulations in a period of some minutes'.[17] According to this aesthetic, just as the virtuoso must abandon virtuosity, the composer of instrumental music must, in the cause of universal taste, embrace vocal music as a model and imitate its more static affect, portraying in a movement a single precise sentiment in much the same way that an aria expresses a text:

The melody of the instruments should be modelled on that of the voice, and vice versa. The adagio of one corresponds to the cantabile of the other; and although [instrumental melody] does not exactly express words, it should at least seek to paint a specific sentiment . . . The voice and instruments should agree on the same aim; why should they follow a different story?[18]

In the same way that an instrumental melody might thus take on the physical and aesthetic characteristics of its vocal counterpart, orchestration, it is argued, should also be 'natural':

Every sounding body has its own character: the bassoon is lugubrious, the oboe tender, the fife gay, etc. If the arbitrary mixture of instruments damages their natural effect, why does one join them together unnecessarily?[19]

Such reviews in effect propose a shotgun wedding of apparently irreconcilable opposites, prevalent aesthetic theory and instrumental composition, and it is easy today to dismiss the proposal that instrumental music should divest itself of many of its primary characteristics and conform to the aesthetic of vocal music. Jean Mongrédien holds that the domination of aesthetic theory by language models and, in particular, by the theory of imitation was a 'tyranny' and a 'curse' which, as it were, afflicted even the most able minds and resulted in a dangerous misperception of instrumental music. He instances Lacépède, who 'instead of trying to discover wherein its [the symphony's] originality lies . . . constantly sought to define it by reference to something else, to something which it is not and by definition cannot be'.[20] What Mongrédien sees as the essential wrong-headedness of aesthetic theory is conveyed in his remark that 'it might have had formidable consequences for the development of music in France', but ultimately he seems to conclude that such theory is irrelevant to instrumental music since 'fortunately, . . . composers were drawn to follow the taste of the public and respond to its requirements rather than obey the theorists' precepts'.[21]

Yet, however inadequate eighteenth-century aesthetic theory may have been in relation to the complexity of instrumental music, it is none the less part of the history of eighteenth-century instrumental music. Neither is it entirely true that there was an absolute dichotomy between aesthetic theory and instrumental music, nor that the aesthetics of vocal music is irrelevant to public taste. In the review of concertos by Krumpholtz, Duport *et al.* quoted above, it is of interest that there is an assumption that the aesthetic of the reviewer is synonymous with popular taste. Virtuoso display, it is claimed, appeals only to a minority of, implicitly, professional musicians, but does not move either the man of learning or the amateur public. The concertos of Krumpholtz and Duport have a broader appeal than the others listed by virtue of their 'appreciable melody' which is understood by 'untrained ears', that is, the amateur public. It is implied therefore that popular and learned taste both demand 'appreciable melody' or 'beautiful simplicity' rather than virtuoso feats, a point which is expressed more directly in other reviews:

> The most able artists should not be indifferent to the selection of the pieces they play: they should not ignore that the public would prefer melodious music [*musique chantante*] to the most learned and marvellous *tours de force.*[22]

While concert programmes and reports of audience response establish beyond doubt the popular appeal of virtuosity and the genres of symphony, concerto and *symphonie concertante*, learned reviews advocating the principles of simplicity and natural melody also claimed to represent a universal popular taste. In effect popular taste was the battleground for the competing claims of learned aesthetic theory and popular instrumental practice.

The aesthetics of simplicity and nature remained contemporary issues in the 1780s and impinged on popular and critial opinion and the consciousness of composers in many ways. Many of the aesthetic arguments of the 1750s were rehearsed anew in the late 1770s, when the *Querelle des Gluckistes et Piccinnistes* gave a new lease of life to old arguments, and the popularity of Gluck's operas in Paris makes the point that the aesthetic of which they were a product was not only the concern of theorists. Connections between the world of opera and its aesthetic and the great Parisian public concerts are plentiful. Le Gros, who as director of the *Concert spirituel* from 1777 presided over the growing popularity of Haydn's music, was the *haute-contre* in the title role of Gluck's *Orphée* (1774). Pergolesi, an icon for the protagonists of learned taste, whose opera *La serva padrona* sparked off the *Querelle des Bouffons*, was also the composer of the Stabat Mater setting which enjoyed enduring popularity in the *Concert spirituel* as an example of the confluence of learned taste and popular appeal.

The reception of Haydn's music in Paris and Haydn's own views on music are also closely related to the poetics of melody and simplicity. It will be remembered that Haydn's first popular success at the *Concert spirituel* was his Stabat Mater, where the model for its evaluation was the setting by Pergolesi, the epitome of 'une grande expression' and 'une grande simplicité', admired above all for its 'chant simple & noble'. The qualities which were recognised in the Stabat Mater settings of Pergolesi and Haydn, which were adjudged lacking in Beck's, were simplicity and the appropriateness of the music to the expression of the text, the values at the heart of eighteenth-century aesthetics. In the opinion of Parisian critics Haydn's Stabat Mater was 'so well felt, the expression so true, the only [one] which could hold up next to that of Pergolèse', and these are the same values which Haydn held in writing the piece, as is clear from his correspondence which mentions the approval which the work received from Hasse:

> You will recall that last year I set to music with all my power the highly esteemed hymn, called Stabat Mater, and that I sent it to the great and world-celebrated Hasse with no other intention than that in case, here and there, I had not expressed adequately words of such great importance, this lack could be rectified by a master so successful in all forms of music. But contrary to my merits, this unique artist honoured the work by inexpressible praise, and wished nothing more than to hear it performed with the good players it requires.[23]

That Haydn should hold such values in connection with vocal music is perfectly understandable, but it is also true to an extent that these values informed both the reception of Haydn's symphonies and Haydn's more general 'theoretical *raisonnements*' of composition. Apart from being admired for its 'grand effects' and 'brilliant gestures', Haydn's music is repeatedly characterised in reviews as charming, graceful and intelligible. In the review of a Guénin symphony quoted in Chapter 2, the symphonies of Haydn's imitators appear confused from the perspective of learned taste ('in accumulating extraordinary modulations, in cutting up phrases, in favouring strange and even baroque melodies'), and lack the distinguishing characteristic of Haydn's music: 'but M. Haydn's

style is full of grace and of the choicest melody'. For those writers com
mitted to the values of vocal music, the acceptable face of instrumental
music was to be found in those works which, for all their complexity and
brilliance, forged a link with learned taste through 'appreciable
melody'. There was an expectation that Haydn's symphonies would
display the 'grâce de chant', and its absence was seen as uncharacter-
istic:

> Among the large symphonies, one admired one by M. Jansson senior, who
> unites very beautiful effects with a noble and vigorous melody. Those of
> M. Hayden produced no less a sensation than usual; but one did not find
> his grand and spiritual touch, that graceful melody, that so ingenious
> joining of ideas which sets him apart, in the new symphony presented
> under his name.[24]

Given the dichotomy between learned aesthetics and instrumental
music, what emerged tentatively in the writerly traditions of the second
half of the eighteenth century was the notion that within the corpus of
instrumental music was a sub-category of works which somehow pre-
served or re-invented, to an extent, the aesthetic qualities of vocal music.
In Parisian criticism this notion was exemplified, first and foremost, by
reference to the works of Haydn, but the critical acceptance of other
composers or works is also couched in such terms. Certain concertos
were more acceptable than others by virtue of their 'appreciable melody';
the Janson symphony mentioned in the above review was perceived as
uniting 'very beautiful effects with a noble and vigorous melody'; and a
Viotti *symphonie concertante* was praised because it joined 'to the rarest
performing talent that of pleasing, original composition, and . . . never
allows one to forget the beauty of melody in even the most learned and
mannered passages'.[25]

The tendency to justify instrumental music by reference to the aesthetic standards of vocal music is not to be found only in the Parisian
press: it is, for instance, central to the aesthetic underpinning the trea-
tises on performance by Quantz and C. P. E. Bach. In relation to the
present discussion, it is of interest that Haydn's 'theoretical *raisonnements*', as reported by Griesinger, begin with the statement that 'a
piece of music ought to have a fluent melody'. Haydn also criticised those
composers who 'had never learned to sing', and his assertion that

'singing must almost be counted among one of the lost arts, and instead of song they let instruments dominate' is absolutely consistent with learned taste.

It should be allowed that in writing about his music, as distinct from composing it, Haydn was adopting the theoretical stance of a prevailing writerly tradition. It has been pointed out by David Schroeder that, in the priority given to vocal music (operas, oratorio and the Stabat Mater) in his 1776 autobiographical sketch, Haydn 'assumed the position of virtually everyone in the eighteenth century who spoke about music, and this was that vocal music is superior to instrumental music. Furthermore, if instrumental music is to be taken seriously at all, it must be based on melodic material with a vocal quality, which Haydn appears to have believed he was doing in contrast to many of his contemporaries.'[26] Eighteenth-century aesthetic ideas and compositional practice were informed and shaped by very different considerations, the former by philosophical and literary traditions, the latter by generic conventions of style and technique. While there is no consistent correspondence between aesthetic theory and compositional practice, the two traditions on occasion converge in unified theoretical/musical statements (as in Gluck's *Orfeo* or the vogue of the *Characterstück* in Berlin in the 1750s), or, more frequently, one tradition appeals, *a posteriori* and selectively, to the other for a theoretical validation of practice or, conversely, for a practical exemplification of theory.

The seemingly inordinate emphasis placed on melody, by Haydn himself and other writers of the eighteenth century, is, in the first instance, of historical rather than stylistic significance. It illuminates the complex nature of the relationship between discourse on music and musical composition, and, however much out of step with twentieth-century views of the importance of eighteenth-century instrumental music, it is none the less an historical fact, in Dahlhaus's explication of the term,[27] which impinged on Haydn's understanding of music and the eighteenth-century reception of his music. It is, of course, entirely natural that the success of Haydn's symphonies in the 1780s should be expressed within the broader framework of eighteenth-century thought. Just as Haydn is acknowledged as a genius, gifted by nature with originality, his music avowedly appealed to both popular and learned taste, to the *savant* and the connoisseur alike, and was admired equally for its 'grands effets' and 'grâce de chant', the touchstones of popular and learned taste. Genius is exemplary and claims the admiration of all; as such it is seen to approach a universal taste.

The importance of beautiful melody in eighteenth-century aesthetics and the perception of the same in Haydn's symphonies are in no sense in conflict with the modern understanding of Haydn's style. Few would argue with the aptness of La Rue's observation that Haydn's themes are in general more remarkable for their motivic make-up and potential for elaboration than for any inherently vocal characteristics.[28] However, the importance which Haydn attached to melody in his writings was arguably more than a nod to a writerly tradition. In the modern literature on Haydn the general observation of La Rue has been qualified in a number of ways: James Webster has highlighted from a stylistic standpoint the occurrence of 'beautiful melodies' in Haydn's so-called *Sturm und Drang* symphonies[29] which are an important legacy for Haydn's later symphonies; and David Schroeder has commented on Haydn's quotation in his symphonies of vocal melodies (from operas, liturgical sources, folksong and street music) which, he argues, aid intelligibility and narrow 'the apparent gap between theory and practice'.[30] I will argue in connection with the 'Paris' Symphonies that in addition to Haydn's characteristic thematic-motivic constructions these symphonies also witness a high instance of melodies which are compatible with Rousseau's notion of natural music and with other eighteenth-century writers' concept of 'beautiful melodies'. This rich seam of apparently naive or pastoral melodies has especial expressive meaning from the perspective of eighteenth-century aesthetics and highlights Haydn's 'grâce de chant', an important aspect of his late symphonic style, which was more apparent, or of greater significance, in the eighteenth century than in the predominantly formalistic critique of the twentieth century.

It is not feasible or desirable to re-create the eighteenth-century listening experience, or indulge in the archaeology of musical hearing. Yet we are ill advised to dismiss as irrelevant the apparent dogmatism of the eighteenth-century poetics of simplicity, nature and melody. It reminds us that both eighteenth- and twentieth-century commentaries on Haydn's music are historical interpretations, prisoners of contemporary thought. Haydn's music is used in the twentieth century, as in the eighteenth, as fodder to exemplify and validate contemporary theoretical constructs, and the problematic relationship between aesthetic theory and compositional practice in the eighteenth century is uncomfortably mirrored in the twentieth-century dichotomy between history and analysis.

5

Splendour and beauty
Symphonies Nos. 82 and 86

In the last quarter of the eighteenth century the symphony was, as a genre, increasingly associated with, as Schulz puts it, 'the expression of the grand, the festive, and the sublime', and 'reaches its aim only through a full-sounding, brilliant, and fiery style'.[1] As Elaine Sisman points out, the symphony was described in terms which bring to mind the rhetorical notion of an elevated style.[2] Splendour and an elevated style were particularly associated with a conspicuous Austrian tradition of C major symphonies: the key of C major was in itself often associated with the expression of grand and majestic affects,[3] and C major symphonies were especially associated with the celebration of festive events,[4] reflected in scoring with prominent brass and timpani parts, and in the employment of fanfares and other gestures appropriate to festive occasions. Throughout his career Haydn provided many spectacular examples of festive symphonies, including a number of earlier symphonies, and each of the late Haydn symphony sets contains a C major symphony (No. 82 in the 'Paris' Symphonies, No. 90 in the second set for the Comte d'Ogny, and No. 97 in the 'London' set). Mozart's 'Jupiter' Symphony is also, of course, a *locus classicus* of this type.[5] The C major festive symphony took some of the conspicuous traits of the symphonic genre as its special character: the elevated splendour associated generically with the symphony became in some C major symphonies the very subject of the symphony.

In the first movement of Symphony No. 82 the predominantly festive character is not associated exclusively with a particular theme, but in a quite real sense is the idea or *sujet* which according to Haydn's theoretical *raisonnements* it was his endeavour 'to develop and sustain . . . in keeping with the rules of the art'. The first group and transition of the Exposition may be seen in this sense as the complex definition of this idea or *sujet* and

Table 5.1. *Structure of Symphony No. 82, first movement*

EXPOSITION
First Group (tonic)
1–8   *1*   *a*+*b* (1–4, 5–8)   *premier coup* and antithesis
9–20   *2*   fanfare rhythm
Counter-statement/Transition
21–4   *1a*+motif *x*   partial counter-statement
25–32   *1a*+*x*
33–59   *1a*+*x*+inversion of *1a*+fanfare rhythm (*2*);
         ending with cadence figure *y* (51–9)
Second Group (dominant)
60–9   *3*+*z*   Introductory phrase (over supertonic pedal), ending with
                   cadence   figure *z* (67–9)
70–83   *4*   Main thematic, textural, and dynamic contrast
Closing Group
84–102   *5*

DEVELOPMENT

103 – 116	117 – 141	142 – 173
1b+*2*	*1a*+*x*, ending with *z*	*4* ending with *y*
V/IV–IV – V/v	v – V/vi	VI♯ – V/V – V

RECAPITULATION
174–81   *1a*+*b*
182–96   *2* (extended)
Transition
197–216 *1a*, ending with *z* (197–213=33ff.; 214–16=67–9)
Second Group
217–30   *4*
Closing Group
231–48   *5*
249–61   *2*

its elaboration, in keeping with the grammatical function of these sections in sonata form, that is, the presentation of a (musical) theme or
themes and the modulation to the dominant. Musically the unity of
character is established with absolute clarity in a tripartite initial paragraph (bars 1–20): the *tutti* arpeggio tremolo figure (*1a*, bars 1–4: see
Table 5.1), presented *fortissimo*, staccato and in unison, is the quintes-

Ex. 5.1 Symphony No. 82/i, bars 1–13

sential *premier coup*; its continuation in bars 5–8, lyrical, legato, con-trasted in texture and *piano*, defines the character of the work by stating its antithesis;[6] and this allows the following *tutti* section (*2*, bars 9–20), dominated by fanfare rhythms and again predominantly unison, to emerge *ex abrupto*, enhancing orchestral splendour with surprise. The obvious affective similarity of the *premier coup* and the fanfare gestures is further emphasised by a shared melodic outline (see Ex. 5.1). Sisman comments that after the half cadence on the dominant (bar 20) 'the opening idea is then recast, piano and with a counterfigure, ultimately leading to the modulatory transition'.[7] While such a description accu-rately reflects its musical grammar in sonata form, the music is much more remarkable for the coherence with which the idea of the first group is elaborated. Between bar 21 and bar 40, three successive presentations of the material of the opening four bars (bars 21–4, a counterstatement in the tonic; 25–32, a sequential passage which launches the transition; and 33–40, over a dominant pedal) elaborate on the character of the first group, each, as it were, comprehending and responding to the details of previous presentations. Thematically bars 21–4 repeat the material of bars 1–4 but *piano* and transformed texturally, akin to bars 5–8 in charac-ter; and an important new rhythmic motif (*x*) is added in place of the abrupt silences of the initial presentation. The transition thus begins abruptly, *tutti* and *forte*, like the fanfare of bars 9ff. but with the theme in the bass, and with new striking effects; the syncopated string texture, the

Ex. 5.2a Symphony No. 82/i, bars 21–8

Ex. 5.2b Symphony No. 82/i, bars 33–6

fz accent on the second beats of bars 30–1, and the rhythmic motif *x* of the counter-statement picked up and transformed into a fanfare-like gesture. The third presentation returns to the tremolo version of the opening but with significant additions, in particular where an inversion of the arpeggio figure (*1a*) is played by flutes and oboes and the fanfare character of the rhythmic motif *x* is confirmed by its combination with the fanfare rhythm (*2*) of bars 9ff. (see Ex. 5.2).

The remainder of the transition is less specific in character and less integrated thematically. None the less it maintains the splendour of the opening in a coherent manner, culminating in the striking cadence figure of bars 51–8, where the strident dissonance (with clashing A♭s and Gs) would no doubt qualify as what Parisian critics regarded as a Haydnesque 'grand effet d'harmonie'. Typically, this significant detail is elaborated in the subsequent course of the movement. Much of the first 50 or so bars of this movement could be described in Schoenbergian terms as an example of 'developing variation',[8] but thematic unity is but one aspect of a more general unity of character. This unity does not preclude contrast; rather, it relies on it. In the first group and transition of Symphony No. 82/i the basic idea, *sujet* or character is sustained against a background of fairly constant textural and dynamic change (in terms of C. G. Körner's theory of character, there is 'something constant . . . implied against which to project change'):[9] the characteristic splendour of the *tutti* scoring is twice interrupted by *piano* sections, and the first thematic idea is constantly modified texturally and acquires new counter-melodies and fanfare figures.

Charles Rosen has pointed out that there is a high incidence of monothematic sonata-form movements in the 'Paris' Symphonies.[10] Yet it is also true that strong thematic contrast plays an increasingly prominent part in Haydn's sonata-form movements from the late 1770s and 1780s,[11] and it appears to be Haydn's strategy that movements which have a particularly striking character in the first group, and a rigorous elaboration of the first group in the transition, require an especially stark contrast in the second group. The most overt contrast of the movement is the thematic dualism between the the first group and the second-group theme which appears at bar 70. The latter is one of a relatively large number of melodies which occur in this symphony and in others of this set which by virtue of their naiveté and exaggeratedly simple construction seem easily compatible with the poetics of simplicity, and in tune with Rousseau's characterisation of natural music. The G major theme is texturally simple, homophonic with a clear disjunction between melody and accompaniment. The accompanying harmonies are restricted to tonic and dominant chords in G major, articulated with utmost clarity by virtue of the four-bar tonic and dominant pedal points in the bassoon. The melody itself is diatonic, moving predominantly stepwise, with

Ex. 5.3 Symphony No. 82/i, bars 70–7.

remarkably simple voice-leading and involving large amounts of motivic and rhythmic repetition (see Ex. 5.3). In the Exposition as a whole this theme acts as an antithesis, an interruption of the generally brilliant character of the movement by a short passage of naive or natural melody. Unlike the first group, however, this melody and what it represents is not elaborated upon in the Exposition: both its continuation and much of the closing group of the Exposition reassert the festive nature of the movement. It functions affectively (that is, as the statement of an opposite without ever threatening to displace the predominant character) in the Exposition as a whole in much the same way as bars 5–8 do in relation to bars 1–4 and 9–20; and to some extent, in the closing section, as bars 84–6 and 89–91 function in relation to bars 87–8 and 92–3.[12]

There is a clear correlation between the basic idea and its antithesis and formal function in the Exposition. Although the formal conventions of a development are less clearly defined, the characters of basic idea and its antithesis are inextricably implicated in shaping this section. In other words, the nature of the content is crucial to the impact of the formal manipulation. The Development section unfolds in three clearly defined paragraphs each beginning *piano* with, in turn, the cadential figure (*1b*) of bar 5 (bar 103), the *piano* version of the first four bars (*1a*) which occurred as a counter-statement at bar 21 (bar 117), and the second-group melody (*4*) of bars 70ff. (bar 142). In the first two paragraphs the four-bar *piano* openings give way to further elaboration of *tutti* festive themes, the fanfare idea (*2*) in the first case and the *premier coup* (*1a*) in the second case. It is in the second paragraph that the most thorough elaboration occurs, with the addition of further detail to the textural elaborations of the transition: for instance, the inverted arpeggio counter-melody introduced in bar 34 is used now in connection with the texture of bars 25ff. (bars 125–30), and the same counter-melody is expanded in bars 131ff. with imitation between oboes and bassoons. While the affective and textural contrasts of the Development are the same as those established in the Exposition, the harmonic range is, of course, much wider. None the less there is a clarity to the tonal planning of the Development which, together with the dynamic and affective contrasts, defines the three paragraphs of the Development. The first paragraph moves from F major to a half cadence in G minor. The second paragraph is centred on G minor but cadences on V of A minor, so, at the beginning of the third paragraph, the affective contrast of the cadence figure and the second-group melody is strengthened by the modal change, A minor to A major. The tonicisation of A major by the eight-bar statement of the second-group melody in turn launches the retransition, a free imitative treatment of an idea from the second-group theme articulating a cycle of fifths leading to a dominant pedal emphasised by the stridently clashing A♭ and G (y) heard first in bar 51.

This account of the first movement has stressed the relationship between the nature of the content and form, yet it is undoubtedly true that much of the genius of the movement as a whole must be understood as Haydn's manipulation of the conventions of sonata form; Haydn, as it were, giving the rule to his art. In the Recapitulation the affective contrasts of the movement are restated, albeit more concisely and with an increased emphasis on the festive material. In formal terms, however, the Recapitulation is, typically, a thorough re-invention of the Exposition rather than a mere restatement with the conventional tonal adjustment;[13] the thematic material is developed anew responding to the previous developments rather than to the initial forms of these materials, and further elaborations are introduced. For instance, the restatements of first- and second-group themes and the closing theme are enriched motivically and/or re-orchestrated. In the substantially rewritten transition the *premier coup* has a new formulation, in which the tremolo arpeggio figure (*1a*) is heard simultaneously with its inversion for the first time, and the fanfare rhythm (*2*) receives an even more splendid orchestration (bars 197–202). The answering phrase in the closing theme (*5*) is recast as an inversion of its first phrase, and again the festive character is enhanced by the new addition of the fanfare rhythm (*2*) on timpani (bars 231–8; cf. bars 84–91). The contrasting second-group theme (*4*) is newly orchestrated with horn pedal points and with the first violin melody doubled, in a favourite Haydn combination, by bassoon (bars 217–24).

In the substantial recasting of the transition, both the partial counter-statement and the first elaboration of the *premier coup* of the Exposition are omitted, so that an expanded treatment of the fanfare (bars 181–93) elides with the second elaboration of the *premier coup* in the Exposition. In the Recapitulation, at the end of the transition the cadence figure (*y*) of bar 51 is omitted, and the theme of bars 60ff (*3*) is also ignored except for its cadence figure (*z* at bar 214). This last omission confirms the pro-visional nature of the theme *3* in the Exposition:[14] its cadence figure (*z*) is however of importance structurally, since it prefaces the main contrast-ing theme of the second-subject group on each of the three times it appears. In the Recapitulation as in the Development, the cadence figure is, however, divorced from its initial context as the closing figure for the theme of bars 59ff.

While these omissions in the Recapitulation by comparison with the Exposition are indicative of the generally greater conciseness of the Recapitulation, there are also a number of areas of expansion. Just as the cadence figure of bar 51 (*y*) is a significant detail in the Exposition which is expanded in the retransition of the Development at bar 162, the momentary G minor inflection in the closing theme of the Exposition (*5* at bar 93) is realised in a cameo-like elaboration of the cadential figure into a brief point of imitation in C minor (bars 239–47). This C minor is resolved to C major in the new Coda, the apotheosis of the fanfare theme, which from bar 255 becomes a simple arpeggiation of the C major triad, *tutti* and with fanfare rhythms in brass and timpani, in the clearest evoca-tion of the festive character of the movement.

The notion that a work should have a consistent character is problem-atic in relation to multi-movement works such as symphonies, which contain manifold contrasts: movements of different tempo, contrasting affect, thematic material and often (in the case of slow movements and minuets and trios) differentiated orchestration. In Symphony No. 82 the Menuet is most obviously influenced by the festive character of the first movement, it is clearly distinguished in character from a courtly dance genre. Unlike other minuets in the 'Paris' Symphonies, this movement has very little thematic development, the modulation to the dominant in the first part of the binary structure is uncomplicated, and the tonal range of the second period (bars 15–26) is very limited (it returns immediately to C major, and perfunctory two-bar sequences lead to the reprise). Lacking any thorough-going thematic or tonal argument, the Menuet gives the impression of an emphasis on the nature of the material itself rather than on its manipulation. This material is presented in a principal ten-bar phrase and a four-bar closing phrase, and these phrases represent the principal contrast of the movement. The ten-bar phrase, *tutti* and *forte* with prominent trumpets and drums, is a splendid expansion of a simple tonic triad arpeggio, rising in pitch, the apex of which is marked by the more insistent reiteration of tonic and dominant notes by trumpets and drums in bars 5–8. The closing four-bar phrase is a lyrical oboe solo, contrasted with the principal phrase texturally, dynamically, rhythmically and melodically. The relationship between the principal phrase of the Menuet and the festive character of the first movement is self-evident, but the definition of the festive character by stating a subsidiary lyrical antithesis is also a strategy common to both Menuet and first movement.

In a symphony with outer movements of brilliance and splendour, in which even the minuet is festive, the slow movement presents problems from the perspective of the symphony's unity of character. Schulz admits as much in his description of the symphony:

> The Andante or Largo between the first and last Allegros has it is true not nearly so certain a character, but is often of agreeable or pathetic or sad expression. However it must have a style that is appropriate to the dignity of the symphony.[15]

Slow movements, in general, contrast starkly with outer movements, yet the slow movement of Symphony No. 82 is arguably 'appropriate to the dignity of the symphony' in a quite specific way. First, the F major theme in this set of double variations is, even more so than the G major theme at bars 70ff. in the first movement, beautiful in the sense of natural and simple: the basis of much of the movement is therefore similar in its aesthetic appeal to other such themes elsewhere in the symphony which act

Ex. 5.4 Symphony No. 82/ii, bars 1–8

as an antithesis to the festive character, except that in the second movement this character dominates. Secondly, a new and more specific
characterisation of this melodic type emerges in the Coda of the second
movement, which in turn is related to the character of the Finale. The F
major theme itself is in many ways the quintessential natural melody. In
the first phrase, four of the eight bars are pure melody, unaccompanied;
the only homophonic texture occurs at the cadences of bars 3–4 and 7–8,
which employ exclusively tonic and dominant harmonies (see Ex. 5.4).
The theme as a whole is characterised by a melody-dominated texture
and a clarity and simplicity of harmony: for instance, six of the eight bars
which constitute the reprise of the first phrase in the second part of the
binary form have a dominant pedal. It possesses a regular structure of
eight-bar phrases (8:‖:8+8, 8), and the first four bars provide the rhythmic patterns for the whole 32-bar theme with the exception of bars 22–3.
Such a theme fits Rousseau's characterisation of 'natural' music and is
typical of the type of 'beautiful melody' which Webster describes as first
emerging in Haydn's *oeuvre* in his *Sturm und Drang* symphonies and
which becomes 'a normal resource of his symphonic style' from the late
1770s and early 1780s, especially as the second, contrasting, theme of
first movements and, as here, in slow movements.[16]

With this and the *minore* theme Haydn constructed a typically sophisticated set of double, or alternating, variations, with a number of varied
reprises and an extensive coda (see Table 5.2). The F minor theme is,
typically, related to the major theme, in this instance by shared rhythmic

Table 5.2. *Structure of Symphony No. 82, second movement*

A	a:‖:b	a'				F major
(1–32)	8:‖:8+8,	8				
B	c:‖:d	c'				F minor
(33–60)	8:‖:12,	8				
A'	a, $v.r.$* of a, b	a'				F major
(61–100)	8, 8,	8+8, 8				
B'	c:‖:d	c'				F minor
(101–28)	8:‖:12,	8				
A²	a, $v.r.$ of a, b	a'				F major
(129–68)	8, 8,	8+8 8				
Coda	b'	e,	f,	a,	e'	F major
(169–217)	6	10,	8,	11,	14	
		(6+4)		(6+4+4)		

*$v.r.$ = varied reprise

patterns. It is also characteristic of *minore* themes, and of first variations in strophic sets,[17] to employ strong contrasts in dynamics and orchestration. The variation of this theme (B') reconstitutes these dynamic and orchestral contrasts in larger phrase-structural units (8, 12, and 8), and an outline of the *minore* theme is accompanied throughout by counterpoint in semiquavers, reminiscent of Fuxian third-species counterpoint. While the variation of the *minore* theme retains the formal repeats and phrase structure, the two variations on the F major theme (A' and A²) replace the formal repeat of the a phrase with a varied reprise and dispense with the formal repeat of the second half of the binary form. Characteristically, the a phrase in the *maggiore* variations first recurs unaltered (except for the doubling of the melody in the bassoon in bars 129–36),[18] and the variation process in the varied reprises of this phrase and of the second half of the theme is confined to subtle re-orchestration (with prominent woodwind solos) and re-harmonisation, with little melodic change or decoration, and with none of the abrupt contrasts and figurative elaboration which characterise the *minore* theme and its variation. The movement as a whole does not rely on the usual repertoire of figurations characteristic of variation movements, yet it contains more contrasts, more changes of texture and orchestral colour and a more flexible structure than occurs in the additive structure of strophic variations.

The truly remarkable features of the movement lie, however, in Haydn's wonderful exploration of a detail of harmonic ambiguity in the theme itself and in the construction of the Coda, the longest in any of the variation movements in the 'Paris' Symphonies. Notwithstanding the fact that the obvious contrast in the movement is the modal interchange between F major and F minor, the tension between F major and G minor is increasingly apparent, culminating in the Coda where it is made explicit. In the F major theme itself, much of the *a* phrase is not harmonised, and although the cadences are emphatically in F major, bars 1–2 and 5–6 of the theme (the unharmonised bars) suggest G minor as much as F major. In the *a'* phrase the implicit G minor is more clearly suggested on two occasions (bars 24–5 and 28–9), albeit over a C pedal point. The suggestion of G minor recurs in the *a'* phrases of A' and A² and also in the varied reprises of phrase *a* (bars 68–9, 136–7, 140–1), so that increasingly one relates the theme to G minor, and consequently, following the *minore* sections at the reprises of the F major theme, a false relation is implied.

The Coda, unlike the rest of the movement, is characterised by varied and sometimes irregular phrase lengths. At its centre is an irregular eleven-bar version of the *a* phrase, which between bars 193 and 197 is harmonised fully in G minor, with the highest note of the phrase (*d'''* in bar 194) harmonised for the first time with a G minor 5-3 chord, and, again for the first time, a chromatic alteration to the melody itself (*f♯''* in bar 195). This unambiguous emphasis on G minor necessitates the compensating three-bar extension of the phrase (the last three bars of the theme, bars 30–2, are expanded to six bars at 198–203) which brings the phrase back to F major. Moreover, this emphasis on G minor is further balanced by the new material, emphatically in F major, which surrounds the 'G minor' phrase in the Coda. The ten-bar phrase *e* comprises three statements of a two-bar unit derived from the rhythm of bars 1–2 of the *maggiore* theme and a further statement which is expanded into a four-bar cadential unit ((3×2)×4). This is followed by an eight-bar phrase (*f*) with altogether new rhythmic and melodic characteristics,[19] and after the G minor phrase the *e* phrase is repeated with a further four-bar extension (see Ex. 5.5).

The two new phrases of the Coda share a number of characteristics:

Ex. 5.5 Symphony No. 82/ii, bars 175–99

both are exaggeratedly naive; both are simple in construction, with an abundance of repetition; and together they comprise eighteen bars of unrelenting alternation of tonic and dominant harmonies, apart from the cadential occurrence of the subdominant in bar 182. These phrases are structurally the clearest possible assertion of the tonic key on both sides of the G minor phrase, but in their naiveté they are also redolent of

Ex. 5.6 Symphony No. 82/iv, bars 1–12

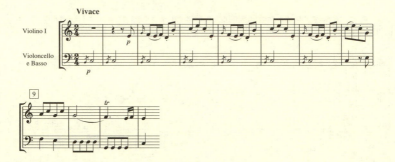

the pastoral or musette *topos*,[20] particularly in the phrase *f* with its emphatic drones.

The simple melodic construction and more specific characterisation in the Coda in the second movement are directly related to the more pronounced pastoral character of the finale. The principal theme of the finale is a ternary structure (*aba'*, with phrase structure 12, 8, 12), and texturally the first and third phrases consist predominantly of a melody and pedal point (see Ex. 5.6). Melodically, each phrase is constructed in the same way as the *e* phrase in the Coda of the second movement, that is, three statements of the same two-bar unit, followed by a cadential extension (only in these cadences of bars 9–12 and 29–32 does Haydn depart from the two-bar melodic idea or from the sparse melody-and-pedal-point texture). Moreover, the pedal point is similar to the drone in the *f* phrase of second movement's Coda (tonic drones with *Vorschläge* in bars 1–8, expanded to drone fifths in bars 22–9), and the middle phrase of the theme (with its wonderfully inventive orchestration of solo oboes accompanied by bassoons, horns and timpani) is restricted harmonically to the use of tonic and dominant chords only. The harmonic, melodic, and textural naiveté of the first 32 bars, together with the drones from which the 'L'Ours' nickname for the symphony derives, creates a specific link between the second and fourth movements, the latter elaborating on the character of the Coda in the former.

It is also typical of Haydn that naiveté of thematic content serves as a foil for compositional complexity of one type or another. In the Coda of the second movement the static F major tonality of the new material serves to highlight the tension between the tonic key and G minor; in the finale the exaggerated use of tonic and dominant harmonies in the main theme gives rise to many of the harmonic surprises of the movement. It is, for instance, a consequence of the nature of the thematic material that modulations in the exposition and development of the finale are often effected, or at least initiated, by the juxtaposition of diatonic passages in different keys, articulated by abruptly shifting drones. After a rudimentary modulation to G major at the end of the first theme (bars 30–2) the normal function of transition begins abruptly and clearly in the dominant with a new drone on D; the tonal juxtaposition is reinforced by a strong textural contrast, and the remainder of the section (bars 33–65) reaffirms the dominant at length. Similarly, the brilliant harmonic surprises at the beginning of the development section involve the juxtaposition of diatonic passages articulated by shifting drones, which suggest A before settling on F major, and G before proceeding in E♭ major (bars 116–18 and 127–30).

For several possible reasons – that the thematic material of the movement involves so much repetition, that even apparently contrasting material in the Exposition is related to the first thematic group,[21] and that the Development section is thematically almost exclusively concerned with the manipulation of the main two-bar idea of the first theme – the Recapitulation of this movement is one of the most radical re-inventions of the material of its Exposition to be found in the sonata-form movements of the 'Paris' Symphonies (see Table 5.3). In all, less than half of the Recapitulation consists of direct restatement or simple transposition of material from the Exposition. After the first twenty bars of the Recapitulation, which is identical with the Exposition, the third phrase of the first group and the first phrase of the second group are omitted, and the new transition is one-third of the length of that in the Exposition. This drastic compression (the first 73 bars of the Exposition are reduced to 32 bars in the Recapitulation) is balanced by the expansion of the second part of the Recapitulation, and overall the Recapitulation (102 bars) is only marginally shorter than the Exposition (115 bars). The two areas of expansion are concerned with forms of the first theme which are not found in the Exposition. Bars 249–63 begin with a new imitative treatment of the main two-bar idea of the first theme and are, motivically and texturally, related to the treatment of the first theme in

Table 5.3 *Symphony No. 82, fourth movement: correspondence between Exposition and Recapitulation*

Exposition			Recapitulation
First Group			
(tonic)			
1	*a*	1–12	179–90
	b	13–20	191–8
	a'	21–33	——
Transition			
		33–65	——
		——	199–209
Second Group			
(dominant)			(tonic)
2	*a*	66–73	——
	b	73–84	210–22
		——	223–35 (new version of *1a*)
	c+a'	85–99	236–49
Coda			
		100–5	——
		——	249–63
		——	264–80 (new version of *1a*)

the development section; the phrase inserted into the second group of the Recapitulation (between *2b* and *2c+a'* at bars 223–35), is a new version of the first theme of the movement, re-forming the two-bar melodic unit into a closed structure (2+2, 2+2) with more prominent cadential articulation. Here and especially in its repetition in the Coda (bars 264–73), this new version of the first theme unites splendour and naiveté in an apotheosis of the pastoral *topos* of the movement, with full *tutti* textures made up of melody and drone fifths and the addition for the final statement of a *fortissimo* drum roll.

Charles Rosen has characterised the achievements of Haydn's mature symphonies as 'heroic pastoral . . . the greatest examples of their kind'. He describes a 'simplicity' and an 'apparent naïveté' which are perfectly compatible with the 'greatest display of counterpoint', with 'the polished surface', and with 'art learned almost to the point of pedantry'.

The pretension of Haydn's symphonies to a simplicity that appears to come from Nature itself is no mask but the true claim of a style whose command over the whole range of technique is so great that it can ingenuously afford to disdain the outward appearance of high art. Pastoral is generally ironic, with the irony of one who aspires to less than he deserves, hoping he will be granted more. But Haydn's pastoral style is more generous, with all its irony: it is the true heroic pastoral that cheerfully lays claim to the sublime, without yielding any of the innocence and simplicity won by art.[22]

The characteristics which Rosen encapsulates in the epithet 'heroic pastoral' are to some extent those glimpsed in the general reception of Haydn's symphonies in the Parisian press of the 1780s, that is, a style which, for all its brilliance and sophisticated craftsmanship, is regarded as graceful, simple and moving. Arguably, however, Symphony No. 82 is illustrative of a heroic pastoral style in a more specific way, in that the consistent character of the work, through all four movements, is embodied in the relationship between two clearly defined *topoi*, which might be described as the festive C major tradition and the musette or pastoral *topos* or, more generally, as uniting splendour and beauty, the popular and learned taste of contemporary criticism. In this sense Symphony No. 82 might be seen as Haydn's quintessential 'heroic pastoral' symphony, in which the unity of character amounts to more than a unity of style and is different in type from the 'intermovemental relationships in Haydn's works' described recently by Webster and Haimo.[23]

Symphony No. 86 in D major is in many ways similar to Symphony No. 82. D major symphonies are allied in character to those belonging to the C major festive tradition, and Symphony No. 86, belonging to an important sequence of related D major symphonies,[24] is the most richly orchestrated of the 'Paris' Symphonies, with prominent parts for both horns and trumpets, and with timpani in three of the four movements. The grandeur of Symphony No. 86 is also evident in its scale, with a slow introduction to the first movement (such as we find in three of the six 'Paris' Symphonies and in most of the Haydn symphonies thereafter), the largest Menuet of the 'Paris' Symphonies, and two substantial sonata-form outer movements.

The first and fourth movements are alike in character and have constructional similarities and common opening strategies: after surprise openings their principal themes, alike in their insistent rhythms, note repetitions and arpeggio outlines, receive *tutti* orchestrations, with insistent horns, trumpets and timpani; and their modulations to the dominant proceed without a change of texture. The principal themes and transitions thus form homogeneous blocks of brilliant orchestral colour (86/i, bars 26–53; 86/iv, bars 9–38), which are all the more effective because they occur *ex abrupto*. In the fourth movement, the effect is almost identical with the opening gesture in the finale of Mozart's 'Paris' Symphony, calculated to stun Parisian audiences – an eight-bar opening, thinly scored and *piano*, followed by a surprise *tutti*.[25] In the first movement the *tutti* statement of the principal theme is delayed much longer and follows a number of other surprises: a 21-bar Adagio introduction, with its own abrupt dynamic changes, and a four-bar off-tonic opening to the Allegro spiritoso (bars 22–5).[26]

Like Symphony No. 82/i, the first and fourth movements of Symphony No. 86 employ strong thematic contrasts in their Expositions, with naive, thinly scored melodic ideas in their second groups in the dominant contrasting with the homogeneous statements of principal theme and transition (86/i, bars 65–73; 86/iv, bars 39–49). Thus in both movements orchestral brilliance is followed by naive simplicity and, as in 82/i, the contrasting themes rely almost exclusively in their harmonisation on two chords, the tonic and dominant. The contrasting themes in 86/i and 86/iv are fragmentary, however; and particularly in 86/iv, with its Lombardic rhythms, chromatic short appoggiaturas, pizzicato accompaniment and (from bar 44) a *buffa*-like orchestration, the themes are more evocative of the comic than the pastoral *topos*.[27] These contrasting themes in the first and fourth movements are also similar in their employment of varied restatements as a constructional feature.[28] In the fourth movement the contrasting theme consists of two six-bar phrases of which the second (bars 45–50) is a varied restatement of the first (bars 39–44). Within each phrase the first two bars are immediately repeated, so that two two-bar ideas with repetition and variation generate the whole twelve-bar period:

a (39–44)	varied restatement of *a* (45–50)
x x y	*x′ x′ y′*
2+2+2	2+2+2

Ex. 5.7 Symphony No. 86/i, bars 62–8

In the first movement the contrasting theme in the dominant (bars
65–73) also consists of two phrases (2+2, 2+4), the second of which
begins as a varied restatement of the first, before an extended cadential
figure; and the first phrase itself comprises two two-bar units the second
of which is a variation on the first.

Typically, such overt contrasts in the character of thematic materials
in these movements are accompanied by unifying features which are
commonly referred to as Haydn's characteristic 'monothematic' sonata-
form procedures. In the fourth movement, the five-quaver anacrusic
figure, which is present for virtually every alternate bar of the first
twenty bars of the first group, is also prominent in the contrasting
material in the dominant (i.e. as an anacrusis to bars 39, 41, 45, 47). In
the first movement the four-bar off-beat start to the Allegro spiritoso
(V^{6-5}/ii–ii, V^{6-5}–I) is restated in the dominant at bar 54 (V^{6-5}/vi–vi,
V^{6-5}/V–V), at the head of an introductory phrase to the contrasting
theme of bars 65ff.[29] In addition, the cadence figure of bars 63–4 foreshadows the 8–5–3 outline of the contrasting theme (see Ex. 5.7), a
connection which seems to be highlighted in the Recapitulation by the
new insertion of an anticipation of this theme before the cadential figure
(bars 186–8), an otherwise inexplicable feature.[30] Such unifying features,
thoroughly typical of Haydn and frequently commented upon in
connection with his music, are perfectly compatible with the overt contrasts, in this instance between the homogeneous first-group/transition
paragraphs and the contrasting, fragmentary second groups.[31]

While the thematic material of these movements is not the most distinguished in Haydn's symphonies, the surface contrasts in texture and
thematic character are enlivened further by the adventurous harmonic
language of this symphony and the occasional display of contrapuntal
wizardry. The abrupt intrusion in the recapitulation of 86/iv of the flat
submediant, resolved to the dominant via an augmented sixth (bars

138–48), reinforces the textural, dynamic and thematic change after the second-group material and is prophetic of the regular and extensive use of the flat submediant at this point in the Recapitulation which characterises many of Haydn's late works. The development of 86/i, notwithstanding its abundance of harmonic surprises and volatile harmonic surface, derived in part from the emphasis on the theme of the off-tonic opening to the Allegro spiritoso which is never stable, is organised in three large paragraphs defined by thematic contrast in a framework of harmonic clarity:

Development of 86/i

86		103	104		125	
1st group (1–4)			1st group (26ff.)		2nd group (65ff.) – 1st group (1–4)	
V^{6-5}/vi		V/iii	iii		V/vi–vi	cycle of 5ths–V

The elaborate Menuet of this symphony shares the pomp, brilliance and elaborate structure of the outer sonata-form movements. After the homogeneous *tutti* of the first phrase, with continuous motivic expansion, a rising tessitura and cadences articulated by brass and timpani, there are two areas of expansion. The first (bars 13–38) consists of two very contrasted phrases. The first phrase (bars 13–20) returns immediately to the tonic over a continuous dominant pedal point and is extraordinarily static melodically and harmonically. The second phrase, beginning in D minor (bar 21), adds an expressive appoggiatura to the main thematic idea of the movement, which is elaborated in a series of chromatic sequences, leading to a dominant pedal at bars 34–8, where the static texture of bars 13–20 returns. This first paragraph of elaboration is *piano* throughout, forming a large 26-bar area of contrast to the *tutti* first phrase and its reprise at bar 39. The reprise itself is twice as long as the first phrase, extended by conventional procedures of periodic interruption, interpolation and repetition.[32] The last four bars of the first phrase are repeated *piano*, with reduced scoring, for the first time interrupting the continuous *tutti* scoring associated with the first phrase, and leading to a deceptive cadence which signals further expansion: the deceptive cadence is followed by the interpolation of four bars of motivic elaboration, and a final presentation of the last four bars of the first phrase.

The Menuet, like the outer sonata-form movements of this sym-

phony, projects the brilliant character associated with D major symphonies against strong contrast. Just as the pomp of the principal themes
in the outer movements have contrasting, naive melodies in their second
groups, the expansive and brilliant Menuet is balanced by a Trio which is
the epitome of graceful simplicity. Its eight-bar principal phrase is,
conventionally, more lightly scored than the Menuet (with the Haydnesque doubling of the melody on solo bassoon); it is also notable for its
clarity of phrase structure, its simplicity of harmony and texture, and its
graceful melody. There is little harmonic or motivic elaboration, as the
second phrase returns immediately to the tonic, and after four bars of
diatonic sequences V^7 is prolonged in eight bars of static but colourful
orchestral dialogue before the reprise. In all these regards it is very
similar to the Trio of Symphony No. 85, particularly in the seemingly
over-long prolongation of the dominant which in Symphony No. 85
Rosen finds sublimely witty, 'delightful because it is so absurdly gratuitous'.[33] The Trio appeals directly to the poetics of 'beautiful simplicity',
and the Menuet and Trio as a whole encapsulate the standards of popular
and learned taste.

The 'Capriccio' is, according to Koch, 'distinguished from ordinary
pieces by its freer form, by its less fixed character, and by a looser connection of its ideas'.[34] In Haydn's *œuvre* the designation 'Capriccio',
together with the allied term 'Fantasia', is reserved for movements with a
particularly wide and chromatic harmonic vocabulary and abrupt
changes of affect, often cast in a hybrid form in which variation plays an
important part.[35] The Capriccio of Symphony No. 86 has a framework
with some of the formal conventions of sonata form, but many of the for-
mally defining moments are made ambiguous, as if the point of the
movement were to defeat formal expectation. For instance, although
there are three thematic ideas in the 'exposition' (*a* at bars 1ff.; *b* at bars
9ff., restated in the dominant at bar 20; and *c* at bars 24ff.), all of which
later recur in the tonic, the 'recapitulation' at bar 54 is weakly articulated; between bars 47 and 53 the closing cadential phrase and first theme
of the exposition firmly articulate the submediant, and only by a chromatic sleight of hand in bar 53 is the recapitulation of the first theme in
the tonic key prepared (see Table 5.4). Similarly, after emphatic closure
on the dominant at the end of the 'exposition' (bar 30), three bars of *tutti*
interruption re-establish the tonic for a reprise of the first theme, as if for

Table 5.4. Structure of Symphony No. 86, second movement, Capriccio

First Group			
1–8	*a*	(4+4)	G major
9–12	*b*		
transition			
13–30		based on *b* with cadential phrase *c* (V⁷/♭III–♭III–V/II♯–V/V–V)	
Interruption	30–32		
33–6	*a*		G major
37–40	*a*		ii–V/VII♯
41–46	development of *a*		VII♯–III♯
47–9	cadence phrase *c*		V/vi
50–3	*a*		vi–V⁷
54–7	*a*		G major
58–70	*b*		
71–4	*a*		i
76–84	*b*		I
85–92	cadence figure *c*		I

a formal repeat of the exposition; but this expectation is itself defeated three bars later when the fourth bar of the first theme is re-harmonised, initiating a highly chromatic 'development' section. Both recurrences of the first theme in the tonic (bars 33ff. and 54ff.) are thus problematic in relation to formal expectations, the first a temporary, 'misleading' assertion of the tonic at the beginning of what turns out to be a development section, and the second an unusually weakly prepared articulation of the tonic at the beginning of the recapitulation. Furthermore, within the recapitulation, after the presentation of the second theme and transition in the tonic (bars 58–68), the first theme recurs in G minor (bars 71–2), necessitating a further, more elaborate repetition of the second theme, followed by the cadence phrase (bars 77–84, 85–92), to effect a tonic closure.

Throughout the movement the first theme recurs in surprise keys, functioning more in the manner of a reprise in a C. P. E. Bach ritornello structure than as a first theme in a sonata-form movement;[36] and quite apart from the keys in which this theme begins in each of its occurrences (G major, A minor, E minor, G major, G minor), its harmonisation is altered, particularly in its fourth bar, generating further surprise continuations (e.g. G major ending V/A minor – bars 33–6; A minor ending V/F♯ major – bars 37–40; E minor ending V/G major – bars 50–3). This is consistent with the importance of variation procedures in other capriccios and fantasias by Haydn, and the chromatic re-harmonisations of the first theme in this movement are also an anticipation of Haydn's more consistent use of this practice in his late string quartets, symphonies and piano trios, famously in the variation movement of 'Emperor' Quartet, Op. 76, No. 6 (cf. the theme and last variation). It is also entirely consistent with Haydn's practice in capriccios that the harmonic surprises mentioned above are emphasised by sudden dynamic and textural changes, as for instance in the *tutti* interruption of bar 25, emphasising the flat submediant of the dominant, or the surprise return to the tonic in bars 30–2, dramatised by abruptly changing dynamics. Thus, the movement as a whole gives the impression of rapidly changing affect, a succession of sudden interruptions and surprises, be they abrupt changes of texture and dynamics, the occurrence of the first theme in unexpected keys, or chromatic twists in the harmonisation of this theme which leads the music rapidly to distant tonalities (as in the modulation from G major to F♯ major in the space of nine bars (33–41).

In character, Symphonies Nos. 82 and 86 are alike in the orchestral brilliance associated with C major and D major symphonies and their countervailing rich seam of naive melody. While lacking any direct references to the pastoral *topos* of Symphony No. 82, the character of Symphony No. 86 also has much in common with other, later, D major symphonies. A London review of Symphony No. 93 referred to Haydn's 'sublime and wanton grandeur',[37] and this rather than the epithet 'heroic pastoral' may ultimately be more appropriate in describing the character of Symphony No. 86. It is not difficult to understand the harmonic surprises, the expansive scale, and orchestral brilliance of Symphony No. 86, especially the first, third and fourth movements, in terms of Kant's description of the mathematical and dynamic sublime;[38] equally, the second movement (Capriccio) of this symphony can be perceived as one of Haydn's most 'wanton' creations.

While in Symphony No. 82 the contrasting characters of the festive symphony and the pastoral *topos* are closely integrated and indeed merge in the finale, in Symphony No. 86 the contrasts are starker, internally in the first, third and fourth movements between the brilliant and the naive or even comic, and in the symphony as a whole between the Capriccio and the other movements. Stark contrasts are not, however, incompatible with the notion of unity of character. Typically, Haydn placed his starkest contrasts, his most wanton creations, in a framework which was intelligible to his audience, a framework which is compatible with contemporary popular taste.

6

Convention and originality
Symphony No. 85

Before the 1790s it is perhaps in Symphony No. 85 – and in Symphony No. 92 from the later set of symphonies for Paris – that Haydn most fully approaches the mature symphonic style of the 'London' Symphonies.[1] Here Haydn draws with ease on a sophisticated musical language, an expanded harmonic range, diverse musical textures, and a formal variety which never lacks complex control. In music history they are seen as the epitome of Haydn's Classical style,[2] a style identified with Haydn's works from the 1780s, with which modern analysis is comfortable. They are also classics in T. S. Eliot's sense of the term, seeming to embody the notion of products of 'a language and a literature [which] are mature; . . . the work of a mature mind'.[3] They seem to stand by Eliot's further criteria for classics as works which are products of an acute 'critical sense of the past, a confidence in the present, and no conscious doubt of the future', and to the modern critic it seems that such works may be appreciated fully as autonomous artefacts without recourse to historical context, the crutch of mitigating historical circumstance, or explication in terms of historical importance rather than inherent worth.

The sophisticated insights which modern analysis brings to the understanding of Symphony No. 85 are not in evidence in eighteenth-century music criticism, but the covert aspects of Classical style emphasised in the former are vaguely acknowledged in the eighteenth century as the ability granted to the genius to transcend convention. If the primary quality of genius is originality and a genius 'gives the rule to art', then modern analysis might be regarded in part as a means of making explicit the relationship between convention and originality as a measure of the eighteenth-century notion of genius, and of elucidating in a purely musical context the more general eighteenth-century notions of unity and coherence.

Table 6.1. Structure of Symphony No. 85, first movement

1–11	Introduction	
First group		
12–22	*1a*	Tonic
23–30	*1b*	
31–41	*1a*	
42–61	Transition (*1b*)	caesura on V/V at bar 61
Second Group		
62–9	*2*	Dominant minor
70–7	*1b*	
78–95	*1a*	Dominant major
96–104	*3a*	
105–11	*3b*	
Development		
112–33	*2*	V/vi–IV
134–71	*1a* (+*1b, 2*?)	♭VII
172–9	*1a*	vi
180–90	*3b*	
191–7	*1b*	
198–211	retransition	caesura on V/vi
Recapitulation		
212–22	*1a*	Tonic
223–37	*1b*	
238–55	*1a*	
256–76	*3*	

Haydn's ability to 'sustain and develop' a single idea, to draw 'rich and varied developments' from a single subject, is apparent structurally in the first movement of Symphony No. 85 in a number of ways. Haimo and Landon have drawn attention to a number of possible motivic links, of varying credibility, between the slow introduction and the material of the Exposition proper,[4] but there are both more obvious and more covert ways in which the musical unity of the movement is manifest. It is in the first instance one of Haydn's most subtly constructed monothematic sonata-form movements, with variants of the first theme (*1a* in Table 6.1) occurring three times in the Exposition and twice in the Recapitulation, and dominating the thematic argument of the Development section. Typically, restatements or transpositions are never (with the exception of the recurrence of bars 78–95 at 238–55) exact, but incrementally new orchestrations, extensions, points of imitation accrue. Thus at bar 31 the restatement is re-scored with the addition of punctuating woodwind chords, and the transposed version in the dominant (bars 78–95) has a new ten-bar chromatic extension and yet another scoring. In the Development section versions of this theme (bars 134ff) have a point of imitation which elides discrete four-bar antecedent and consequent structures into longer phrases, with new refinements of orchestration and the addition of new counter-melodies. Again typically, the recapitulation of the first theme at bar 212 is not a restatement of this material in its initial form; rather, it picks up on the refinements of the Development section, and a new horn counter-melody appears for the first time.[5] The integration of variation procedures into sonata form is a prominent feature of Haydn's style and is supremely manifest in the first movement of Symphony No. 85.[6] As Jens Peter Larsen has pointed out, the regular recurrence of varied forms of this first theme also affects the shape of the movement in a very fundamental way: varied but thin scorings of this theme, alternating with *tutti* sections, suggest a textural form in some ways more akin to the alternation of ritornello and episode sections in a concerto than to the polarity of strongly contrasted themes associated with some sonata-form models.[7]

The sustained treatment of the first theme is the most obvious unifying feature of the movement, but the movement is integrated in other subtle ways, the most striking being associated with Haydn's ingenious play with the conventions of sonata form, specifically, his defeat of the listener's expectations at three structurally significant points: the beginning of the dominant area of the Exposition; the beginning of the Development section; and the retransition. In Haydn's mature sonata forms the secondary tonal area of the Exposition is increasingly characterised by some degree of local chromaticism or instability. In the case of the first movement of Symphony No. 85 the displacement of the expected dominant major key takes place at the beginning of the section and is particularly striking: a perfectly conventional caesura on V/V at bars 60–1 is followed by an extended passage in the dominant minor, its shock effect being reinforced by the *fortissimo* dynamic (where a more lyrical *piano* theme might be expected) and by the fact that the thematic material bears a striking resemblance to the opening of the 'Farewell' Symphony (*2* in Table 6.1).[8] No less impressive than this striking defeat of expectation is the manner in which in the following passage the minor mode and the 'Farewell' theme effortlessly evolve into a statement of the first theme (*1a*) in the dominant major key. The 'Farewell' theme (*2*) is succeeded by theme *1b* without a change of texture, but the latter is in an altered form which anticipates the return of the first theme (*1a*). Its characteristic scalic anacrusis is present (bars 70, 72, 74), but the staccato crotchets outline a conjunct descending fourth (as opposed to the earlier disjunct arpeggio outline at bars 24ff. and 42ff.), and this is played in parallel thirds by first and second violins in the manner of the first theme. This motif is the constant feature in bars 70–8 as the anacrusic figure of *1b* is dropped, the staccato crotchets are transformed to quavers followed by quaver rests, the dynamic is altered from *forte* to *piano*, and the mode changes from minor to major. Thus by a succession of changes in detail the abrupt thematic and harmonic interruption of the 'Farewell' theme is dissipated. The manner in which characteristics of initially distinct themes merge here is also part of the thematic manipulation of the Development section (see in particular bars 134–71).

The beginning of the Development section is, in Haydn's mature sonata-form movements, always liable to contain unconventional features, in particular, bold harmonic *coups* which challenge the listener's expectations. By comparison with conventional mid-eighteenth-century practice of beginning the Development in the dominant, the dominant minor, or some other closely related key, the relationship between the end of the Exposition and the beginning of the Development in this movement contains a double shock.[9] The dominant (F major) ending of the Exposition is followed by D major[7], an abrupt mediant juxtaposition, radical in this context although increasingly familiar in Haydn symphonies, and a further defeat of conventional expectations occurs with the deceptive resolution to E♭ major (V:II:V[7]/vi–IV), in which key the 'Farewell' theme reappears. Thus for the second time in the movement the 'Farewell' theme is associated with a harmonic surprise; moreover, the opening of the Development on V[7]/vi foreshadows the single most unusual feature of the movement, namely, the unconventional retransition section of bars 191–211, which

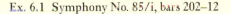

Ex. 6.1 Symphony No. 85/i, bars 202–12

emphasises V/vi and articulates the Recapitulation in a wholly unconventional manner.

From bar 191 to the Recapitulation at bar 211, D major (V/vi) is strongly emphasised, with a continuous D pedal point and a melodic outline which stresses the D major triad; indeed the motivic treatment of the theme *1b* (in the version which was previously heard at bars 71–5) is reduced, from bar 205 onwards, to repetitions of the D major triad. It would at this point be conventional to have a resolution to the submediant, from which point in much eighteenth-century music the retransition is launched.[10] Instead Haydn elides V/vi with the tonic key and the reprise of the first theme, with only the slimmest of melodic links, a one-bar melodic descent ($d''-c\sharp''-c\natural''$), and the usual elaborate dominant preparation is entirely omitted (see Ex. 6.1).

The articulation of the Recapitulation is one of the most important and dramatic events in a sonata-form movement, one usually signalled to the listener well in advance of its arrival and often the climax of the movement. In Galeazzi's description of sonata form it is stressed that 'however remote the Modulation is from the main key of the composition, it must draw closer little by little, until the Reprise, that is, the first Motive of Part I in the proper natural key in which it was originally written, falls in quite naturally and regularly'.[11] Haydn's failure to resolve the emphatic stress on V/vi at this point in the movement can be understood only as a deliberate play with conventional expectation. Jan La Rue has characterised this procedure as 'bifocal' tonality,[12] Haydn's unconventional recasting of a progression associated with Baroque music within the syntax of sonata form; and more recently Ethan Haimo has referred to this moment as 'a purposeful and powerful anomaly – unresolved, unexplained, and not otherwise followed up within the first movement itself'.[13]

Ex. 6.2 Symphony No. 85/i, bars 1–3

The striking harmonic progressions at the beginning and ending of the Development are, however, not isolated details, individual shocking effects without preparation or consequence; rather, they are prepared in the harmonic ambiguity of the first three bars of the introduction to the first movement and ultimately resolved in the finale.[14] In the introduction a B♭ root-position tonic triad is stated for the first time in bar 4, and in the first three bars conflicting signals are given to the listener. The B♭ octaves of the opening chords emphasise the tonic, but on the first beats of bars 2 and 3 G and E♭ are stressed; the G a *tenuto* minim, the longest note in the first three bars, the E♭ because it is the only chord sounded in the predominantly unison texture of these bars. Between the first beats of bars 1–3 emphasising the outline B♭–G–E♭, the more animated dotted rhythms contain chromatic inflexions suggesting G minor more than B♭ major, and each of the latter outlines a D major triad. The bass progression B♭–G–E♭ foreshadows the melodic outline of theme *1b* (bars 23–8);[15] the abruptly introduced E♭ major in bar 3 foreshadows the manner of the occurrence of the 'Farewell' theme in E♭ major at bars 114ff.; and arguably the chromatic inflexions of the dotted rhythms in bars 1 and 3 lead one to hear the implied harmony of bars 3–4 as V/vi–I, a hint of the importance of this progression in framing the Development section and of the ellipsis or 'bifocal' effect at the end of the Development (see Ex. 6.2).

These features are unresolved details in the first movement which arguably necessitate a balancing over-emphasis on dominant preparation elsewhere in the work, specifically, in the Trio of the third movement, bars 52–70, and in the preparation for the final reprise in the finale, bars 146–63. In the Trio the principal eight-bar phrase and routine modulation are absurdly over-balanced by nineteen bars of dominant preparation:[16]

$$a:\|:b \qquad a$$
$$8:\|:5+19 \quad 8$$

Table 6.2. Structure of Symphony No. 85, fourth movement

1–24	A	Tonic	*a*:‖:*ba*
25–69	B	I	*c*
		V	*d*
			e
			d'
70–84	A	I	*a b*
85–163	C	developmental episode	
		retransition V/vi–vi–V (130ff.)	
164–89	A	I	*a b a"*
190–220	Coda	I	*d d"* (=a?)

In the finale the central developmental episode recalls the first movement in its emphasis on G minor and particularly the rhetorical stress on V of G minor at bar 130.[17] However, unlike the ellipsis from V/vi to I in the first movement, the modulation from G minor to the tonic is elaborately worked out in the finale (bars 138–63): the bass descent to the dominant pedal is completed, and in the upper voices there is an elaborate descent (*b♭"–e♭"* in bars 138–46, and *e♭'''–f"* in bars 148–63, the latter as part of an 18-bar passage of dominant-seventh harmony articulating the reprise in a clearly parodistic manner). Here Haydn with supreme wit parodies the very convention which he flouted in the first movement, projecting as a large-scale unifying feature between movements a harmonic detail which is in the first instance prominent in relation to contemporary formal conventions.

Apart from this passage, the finale is in other ways an exemplification of Haydn's genius, in the eighteenth-century sense, in that its overall structure is a typically Haydnesque conflation of formal conventions. At first it appears to be a typical rondo finale, with a characteristic 2/4 rondo theme in rounded binary form and a macrostructural organisation like many another rondo (see Table 6.2). Unlike sonata-form movements it lacks a repeated exposition, and the rondo refrain returns in the tonic after the first episode, a defining feature of rondos as distinct from sonata-form or hybrid sonata-rondo forms. It shares none the less many features of Haydn's sonata-form movements. It is assiduously mono-thematic in construction, in that the three 'new' phrases of the first episode share a head-motif from the refrain, and the second episode is as rigorous a development section as in any sonata-form movement. Haydn is also free in his treatment of the refrain material, which is drastically shortened on its first recurrence, and the second recurrence has characteristics of a recapitulation in sonata form. After a shortened presentation of the refrain material *per se*, reference is made to the inevitable counterpoint of the first refrain recurrence (bars 182ff, cf. bars 86ff), before the dominant phrases of the first episode are recapitulated in the tonic (bars 189ff, cf. bars 39ff). Thus despite the obvious rondo characteristics of the movement, a defining feature of sonata-form movements is incorporated (i.e. the recapitulation in the tonic of material associated with the dominant), and there is a subtle cross-reference between refrain and episodic materials rather than literal reprises of the refrain in its initial form (for instance, the second recurrence of the dominant phrase d'' at bar 204 more closely resembles the a refrain phrase, emphasising the near identity of a and d). This movement therefore exhibits at many levels the dual characteristics of unity and sophisticated play with convention which characterise the whole work.

Haydn's genius for play with inherited convention is most apparent in the original treatment of the formal conventions in the first and fourth movements of Symphony No. 85, and it is such movements that are often stressed in modern discussions of Haydn's mature Classical style. From this perspective, slow movements, particularly those in strophic variation forms, and minuets are often less obviously original and are relatively neglected in the modern literature. Given their additive structure and lack of large-scale structural dissonance, harmonic conflict and resolution, the apparently static form of variation movements is often an embarrassment to critics who emphasise the undoubted originality of Haydn's more dramatic forms.[18] Straightforward strophic sets of variations, in particular (even the most sophisticated movements in Haydn's mature works), are often viewed as conservative from the perspective of the history of forms, either in relation to Haydn's characteristic double-variation or hybrid-variation movements, or by comparison with later variation forms, particularly those of Beethoven. Charles Rosen, for instance, while acknowledging that Haydn 'attempted a new approach to variation-form in his double variation-sets', views these forms as essentially static and decorative by comparison with the 'radical change' of

Beethoven's variations.[19] In Ethan Haimo's analysis of Symphony No. 85 the extensive discussion of unity in the outer movements is in contrast to the single paragraph devoted to the second movement.[20] Similarly, in discussing the Menuetto and Trio Haimo's emphasis is on the large-scale harmonic connection between this and the outer movements, rather than on the movement *per se*, which has 'rather straightforward [compositional] premises', and 'seems very ordinary'.[21] None the less, even as regards structure these movements too have a number of notable features.

In the second movement, the *minore* variation, characteristically the second of the four variations, treats the theme more freely, departing from its melodic outline in the first part, and from the phrase structure of the second part (5+7, as opposed to 6+8). It is also followed by an eight-bar transition passage between the *minore* second variation and the return to the major mode in variation three. The fourth variation is followed by a ten-bar Coda and both contain references to earlier variations: the final bars of the fourth variation (112–16) refer to the dynamic and textural contrast of the first variation at bars 41–3 and the Coda employs a four-bar phrase (bars 117–20, repeated with varied orchestration in bars 121–4), which closely echoes the part-writing and new counter-melody of the *minore* variation. The melodic outline of bars 117–20 is the same as the 'new' melodic outline of the *minore* variation (bars 45–8); the duplication of the melody in parallel sixths in the *minore* variation at bars 47–8, a feature not characteristic of the initial theme, is echoed in the parallel thirds of the Coda (bars 119–20); and the beginning of the new counter-melody of the *minore* variation (first violin, bars 45–6) is present in the accompaniment of the Coda (viola bars 117–18, first violins bars 121–4: cf. Exx. 6.3a and b).

In the Menuetto there is an appearance of conventionality in the main body of the movement itself, which is presented in three regular eight-bar phrases without any significant thematic or harmonic development. As in other minuets in the 'Paris' Symphonies, however, the Coda, more than one-third of the total length of the movement, contains significant elaborations, contradicting Haimo's comment that 'it merely repeats, in slightly varied form, material that was heard in the main body of the Menuetto, with no new motives and no unexpected emphases'.[22] After conventional cadence extensions between bars 24 and 30, the opening

Ex. 6.3a Symphony No. 85/ii, bars 45–8

Ex. 6.3b Symphony No. 85/ii, bars 117–22

eight-bar phrase is compressed into a five-bar lyrical oboe solo (bars 30–4), with the Lombardic rhythms, a striking feature of the original, present only in the string accompaniment.

These features are, however, individual refinements in movements which, in their entirety, are less well appreciated by the criteria of formal

Ex. 6.4a Symphony No. 85/iii, bars 1–8

Ex. 6.4b Symphony No. 85/iii, bars 30–4

complexity and originality than by the learned and popular taste of eighteenth-century criticism. According to Pohl, the theme of the second-movement variation-set is a French folksong, 'La gentille et jeune Lisette', and its melodic, textural and harmonic simplicity is compatible with the eighteenth-century aesthetics of beautiful simplicity.[23] Its elaboration in four variations eschews the overworked eighteenth-century formulae of figurative variations, the 'eternal variations without variety' of one eighteenth-century critic,[24] in favour of variation in texture and orchestration, and restrained decoration. Dynamic and textural contrasts, rather than figurative variations, form the basis of variation one, for instance; and in variation three the theme is stated exactly as in bars 1–22 with a new flute obbligato adding colour, in the manner of stylised birdsong, without compromising the naiveté of the theme. The attraction of the Menuetto is also, in no small part, one of changing orchestral colour. In bars 1– 24 *tutti* and string scoring alternates in eight-bar units, while in the Coda thematic elaboration is characterised by more frequent changes of colour. The cadence extension of bars 24–30 contains smaller units of string and tutti contrasts, while the oboe solo of bars 30–4 is followed by a *forte* closing phrase which itself contains a textural *crescendo* (bars 34–8). Just as the simple theme of the second movement is clothed primarily in restrained decoration and new orchestral colours rather than virtuoso figuration, the transformation of the opening *tutti* phrase of the Menuetto into a pastoral oboe solo in the Coda represents, in a detail, the liaison of popular and learned taste in Haydn's music (cf. Exx. 6.4a and b). In the symphony as a whole, the complexity and originality in the manipulation of formal convention in the outer movements, which has been stressed by modern critics, is balanced by an emphasis on grace and colour in the middle movements, and it is arguably this sense of decorum which explains the broad appeal of Haydn's symphonies to eighteenth-century Parisian audiences.

7

Irony and humour
Symphony No. 83

In the context of the reception of Haydn's symphonies in Paris in the 1780s it is difficult to see how Symphony No. 83 is particularly representative of what David Schroeder regards as 'Haydn's wish to achieve intelligibility in his symphonies'.[1] It is certainly a challenging work, but it is bizarre in the extreme, and by comparison with the other 'Paris' Symphonies, Haydn seems at times to be careless of his listeners. Symphony No. 83 has every appearance of being the most wilful and eccentric of the set. It is not just that, like many another of Haydn's symphonies, it abounds with compositional surprises, rational deceptions which require the participation of the listener; difficulty and eccentricity are celebrated, contrasts are extreme, and the work seems to lack the decorum of the other 'Paris' Symphonies, the concern to place difficulties in an intelligible context.

The first and second movements especially seem to return to a style associated with Haydn's works of the late 1760s and early 1770s, his so-called *Sturm und Drang* style.[2] It is the only minor-key symphony in the 'Paris' Symphonies, and the opening theme of the first movement has many of the characteristics of Haydn's earlier minor-key symphonies. Its regular phrase structure and lack of internal contrast, in bars 1–16 especially, are emphasised by a distinct 'stop–start' effect in which the silences between phrase components (bars 4, 8, 16) are disruptive: they halt abruptly the otherwise insistent measured *tremolando* quavers of the accompaniment, and the contrast of a uniform *tutti* texture and silence is unmediated. The melody of these bars is remarkable for its strident dissonance, most notably the C♯ of bar 2, which emphasises augmented-second and tritone intervals in a parody of the conventional triadic outline of many first themes in symphonies (see Ex. 7.1). The frequent *sforzando* accents and disjunct melodic outline of the first theme are also

81

Ex. 7.1 Symphony No. 83/i, bars 1–4

conventionally regarded as typical of Haydn's earlier minor-key symphonies, and in the first movement as a whole, the extensive contrapuntal
writing of the Development and the extreme thematic contrast within
the Exposition are also consistent with Haydn's earlier style.[3] This latter
point is the most striking of a number of contradictions within the work,
and although other movements in the 'Paris' Symphonies contain thematic dualism within the Exposition (Symphonies No. 82/i and 87/i for
instance), here the contrast in the associated *topoi* is particularly extreme.
Within the fairly continuous *tutti* texture of the first 45 bars there is
already a contrast between the strident first theme and what Schroeder
has characterised as the dance-like *Rutscher* theme of bars 33–41,[4] but
this is preparatory to the strongest contrast and clearest articulation of
the relative major key in association with the famous 'La Poule' theme of
bars 45–59.[5] In contrast to the seriousness of the first theme the 'Poule'
theme is distinctively comic, and the difference in character is emphasised by the lightness of texture, the melodic and harmonic simplicity,
and the large amount of internal repetition.[6] The striking opening of the
movement and the 'Poule' theme represent extremes, between heavy and
light scoring, between dissonance and diatonicism, between seemingly
antithetical *topoi* evocative of the sublime in the first theme and of
comedy in the 'Poule' theme; and this contrast is intensified in the
Development section.

While in the Exposition the contrast between the first theme and the
'Poule' theme is mediated by the *Rutscher* theme and by a modulation
from tonic minor to the relative major key, at the beginning of the
Development section the contrast is intensified. Bars 69–82 seem to
highlight the essential point of the Exposition in that its contrasted *topoi*
are presented in a stark juxtaposition emphasised by a mediant harmonic
relationship (V/iv–VI), and by extreme contrast in dynamic and
scoring, and articulated by an abrupt silence. Such stark juxtapositions

Ex. 7.2 Symphony No. 83/i, bars 59–60

Ex. 7.3 Symphony No. 83/i, bars 83–6

are indeed typical of the Development as a whole, in that the contrasting textural blocks (bars 69–72, 73–82, 83–116, 117–29) also contain different *topoi*. The comic intrusion of the 'Poule' theme is followed by the most serious and archaic-sounding contrapuntal development in the 'Paris' Symphonies (bars 83ff.), in which the first theme and its inversion (oboe, bars 83–4) are combined with a figurative decoration of the latter in a texture resembling Fuxian third-species counterpoint; and the texture of bars 83ff. is inverted in bars 92ff.[7] Similarly, the Recapitulation is articulated by abrupt contrasts: following the *tutti* contrapuntal development of bars 83–116 another abrupt silence, a hallmark of the movement, is followed by a retransition involving a new transformation of the first theme – legato, thinly scored and *piano* – moving sequentially from V/II♯ to the tonic, and allowing the Recapitulation to emerge *forte* and *ex abrupto*.

Overall, this is a movement of strong surface contrasts. It is not, however, without Haydn's usual control and a compositional unity centred on Haydn's inventive powers of thematic transformation. The closing theme of the Exposition (bars 59ff.) is related by inversion to the first theme (see Ex. 7.2), and an augmentation of this inversion is part of the contrapuntal texture of the Development section (oboe, bar 83; see Ex. 7.3). A further transformation of the first theme is introduced in the Development section at the retransition (bar 117), and this reappears in the Coda (bars 182–9). This is the final dramatic *coup* of the movement,

Ex. 7.4 Symphony No. 83/i, bars 182–5

introduced after a fermata on V/V (bar 181) and from bar 184 combined
with the dotted-rhythm, inverted pedal point which is a prominent
characteristic of the 'Poule' theme (see Ex. 7.4; cf. bars 52ff.). While the
Development section opens with the starkest statement of the essential
contrast of the Exposition, the movement ends with a new event, a
gesture of reconciliation, without attempting to resolve or dissolve the
contradictions of the movement.

Like the first movement, the sonata-form Andante is in some ways
reminiscent of Haydn's style of the late 1760s. The opening statement
and varied partial restatement are similar in presentation to the Andante
of Haydn's A flat Sonata, Hob. XVI:46, and the subsequent sequential
and imitative treatment of this theme to fashion a retransition (bars
36ff.) is similar to the first movement of Symphony No. 83 and to
retransitions in the keyboard sonatas of the late 1760s and early 1770s,
for instance Hob. XVI:44/i, bars 46–51. Also like the first movement, it
is a movement of extreme contrasts, particularly in the material associated with the dominant key in the Exposition (bars 23–43). At a local
level, in bars 23–9 there are notable dramatic *coups* in the *forte* outburst of
bar 23, followed by four bars of *sempre più piano* signalling in its stasis an
even more dramatic *fortissimo* interruption. Moreover, in the dominant
material as a whole, the dramatic gestures of bars 23–9, which bring to
mind the 'ombra' *topos* of opera,[8] are contrasted with utterly formulaic
material from bar 30 to bar 41, specifically the melodic descent and
accompanying bass pattern of bars 30–3 and the cadenza formula of bars
35–41. Most of the second half of the Exposition is remarkable for its
dearth of significant melodic interest, its impact relying almost entirely
on gesture. The material of this movement is no less disparate than that
of the first movement, and in the Development and Recapitulation there
is a fast rate of textural change and a succession of interruptions and

juxtapositions of antithetical materials, intensifying the contrasts of the Exposition. Although the Andante is cast in the broad outline of a sonata-form movement, in other respects its character is close to the capriccio and fantasia tradition; its abrupt and rapid changes of affect and its concentration of harmonic surprises and dramatic orchestral gestures, independent of significant thematic statement or development, place it in the same tradition as the Capriccio of Symphony No. 86.

While less overtly dramatic than the first two movements, the Menuet is in keeping with the bizarre character of the symphony as a whole. The first phrase of the Menuet is eccentric in its accentuation, with its initial motif unusually occurring on both first and third beats, creating alternating ternary and binary rhythmic groups and obscuring conventional patterns of accentuation associated with minuets. The reprise of this opening phrase at bar 25 and the codetta at bars 35ff. are also unconventional in different ways; the former in that the melodic reprise of the first four bars is re-harmonised on a dominant pedal, and the latter in that the rhythmic instability of the first phrase is reinforced by the placement of the V–I cadence on the weak second beats (bars 37–42). By comparison, the unusual 12/8 Vivace G major finale is seemingly not in keeping with the character of the symphony as a whole. It is, as Landon has pointed out, evocative of the 'chasse' *topos*,[9] and at the end of the movement the fragmentation of the 'chasse' theme using fermatas (bars 80–8) is typically Haydnesque in its wit. None the less, the lightweight character of the Exposition and Recapitulation is in contrast to the main body of the Development section, which, in its harmonic daring and its relentless, uniform texture, devoid of thematic development, brings to mind the abstract harmonic improvisation of a keyboard fantasia or the qualities of the 'marvellous', the startling harmonies and 'complete uniformity' which Michaelis associated with the sublime.[10] The emphasis on the flat submediant at bars 21–4 and 73–6 and the ending of the Development on the dominant of G minor (bars 51–5) are also reminders of the first movement.

The contradictions stated starkly in the first movement especially are multiplied in the progress of the symphony as a whole. Serious and comic oppositions in the first movement are, as it were, writ large in the progression from the *Sturm und Drang*-like first movement to the 'chasse' finale; a symphony ostensibly in G minor abandons the minor mode as its tonal centre after bar 145 of the first movement. The contradictions of the first movement are also matched in the symphony as a whole by an affective range which is more extreme than in any other symphony in the set. Yet the symphony as a whole is neither a mere hodgepodge of unrelated affects nor a simple return to an eccentric earlier style. Symphony No. 83 can arguably be read, in the first instance, as a symphony of pre-eminent wit and humour and, secondly, as an ironic symphony in which Haydn evokes his earlier style in detached contemplation.

Writing in 1807, Michaelis commented on the 'considerable element of humour in modern music, especially since Joseph Haydn, the greatest master in this genre, set a pattern, particularly in his highly original symphonies and quartets'.[11] He distinguished between different types of humour. The term 'scherzando' is associated with witty and jovial music which has a pleasing character and aims to 'cheer and entertain us'.[12] On the other hand Michaelis recognised an altogether more serious humour, one in which 'impressions conflict strangely with each other' and through which the composer expresses 'the strange succession and transformation of emotions and ideas to which he is subject'.[13] He associates this serious humour with the musical genres of the capriccio and the fantasy, but in finding these qualities pre-eminently in Haydn's symphonies and string quartets Michaelis undoubtedly has in mind the freedom from convention, the rapid change of affect, and the harmonic daring associated with the spirit of the fantasia in the eighteenth century, rather than the specific stylistic characteristics of the keyboard fantasia tradition. Strange or inappropriate juxtapositions associated with the spirit of the fantasia give rise to a higher form of humour which Michaelis invests with the qualities of the sublime; he describes, in a direct reference to Kant's 'Analytic of the Beautiful', the impression given by such juxtapositions as one in which 'the imagination *cannot quite* enjoy free play [my emphasis]', distancing his notion of the 'comic sublime' from Kant's condition for the pure judgement of taste.[14] The impact of such inappropriate juxtapositions was differently acknowledged in earlier writings, as for instance in Voltaire's definition of wit as 'the art either of bringing together two things apparently remote, or of dividing two things which seem to be united, or of opposing them to each other'.[15] Such bizarre juxtapositions – whether understood as representative of Voltaire's wit or of Michaelis's comic sublime – have been since the eighteenth century associated with Haydn's symphonies, and in some instance what was seen as the inappropriate mix of serious and comic elements was the focus of negative criticism of Haydn's music by Hiller and others.[16] Symphony No. 83, undoubtedly the most eccentric of the 'Paris' Symphonies, is in Voltaire's sense also the most extreme in its wit. While the 'Poule' theme of the first movement is humorous in Michaelis's sense of 'scherzando' (i.e. pleasing, jovial and entertaining), it assumes the higher status of serious wit or the comic sublime by virtue of its context, its inappropriateness in a G minor movement which is dominated by the seriousness of the Haydn's *Sturm und Drang*-like rhetoric. Similarly, the dramatic interruptions of the second movement are comic in the context of the following harmonic clichés; the limping unconventional Menuet is humorously clumsy in relation to the graceful dance-like Trio; the Development section of the finale is witty in its inappropriateness, as the finale as a whole is bizarrely inapt in relation to the first movement. In short, the symphony's spectacular displays of bizarre contrasts are emblematic of the comic sublime, stretching the credulity of the listener to an extent that none of the other 'Paris' Symphonies do, even in their most audacious moments.

Many of Haydn's compositional surprises have been interpreted by Mark Evan Bonds as ironic. He writes of Haydn's thwarting of expectation and subversion of convention as the music 'call[ing] attention to its own structural rhetoric' and as betraying 'the presence of the composer within the work' in a way which parallels, for instance, Laurence Sterne's self-conscious and ironic attitude to narrative and the relationship between the author and reader in *Tristram Shandy*.[17] Various other authors have called on irony as a way of characterising Haydn's stock-in-trade play with structure, in the sense that, in relation to convention, Haydn's music may often be seen as having an inner meaning for a privileged listener.[18] This understanding of irony in abstract instrumental music is viable in other 'Paris' Symphonies no less than in Symphony No. 83; the over-emphasis on dominant preparation in the Trio and Finale of Symphony No. 85 is, for instance, in this sense ironic. Symphony No. 83 is, however, arguably ironic in another manner, exemplifying in effect some of the central tenets of Romantic irony, particularly the notions of ironic self-detachment and self-parody.[19] Haydn's reference to his own symphonic style of the late 1760s and early 1770s is more pervasive in the *Sturm und Drang*-like first movement of Symphony No. 83 than in the intertextual reference to the 'Farewell' Symphony in the first movement of Symphony No. 85. Yet it is in no way a return to this earlier style; indeed, for Landon the finale represents 'a deliberate negation of the *Sturm und Drang*'.[20] Rather, Haydn parodies his earlier style, evoking it in an entirely alien context which betrays a compositional self-awareness and, as it were, the composer's detached contemplation of himself in the work. Just as the references to his earlier style are ironic, so too the humour of Symphony No. 83 is entirely serious. More than in any other of the the 'Paris' Symphonies, in this work Haydn seems to foster an elitism of privileged understanding which seems utterly compatible with Friedrich Schlegel's comments on irony in Goethe's *Wilhelm Meister*:

> But we should not be deceived into thinking that the poet is not utterly serious about his masterpiece, even though he himself seems to take the characters and incidents so lightly and playfully, never mentioning his hero except with some irony and seeming to smile down from the heights of his intellect upon his work.[21]

8

The refinement of popular taste
Symphonies Nos. 84 and 87

By comparison with the eccentricities of No. 83, Symphonies Nos. 84 and 87 are distinctly popular in appeal. Both works share a large range of orchestral colours, with a prominence given to woodwind instruments, unequalled in the 'Paris' Symphonies. They contain a number of orchestral mannerisms and melodic types which would have been familiar to Parisian audiences accustomed to the orchestral grandeur of Mannheim symphonies, and both also allude to generic conventions of the concerto and *symphonie concertante* traditions which provided the standard fare of Parisian concerts in the 1780s. They are, in short, symphonies very much in tune with contemporary Parisian expectations of the 'grande symphonie', but, notwithstanding their concessions to popular taste, they could not be mistaken for works of another composer. They adopt the manner and orchestral grandeur of the public symphony of the 1780s but with all the refinements, in harmonic language, formal variety and control, which characterise Haydn's mature symphonies.

It is perhaps significant that, anticipating Artaria's publication of the six symphonies in two sets of three, Haydn, in indicating their ordering to the publisher, placed Nos. 87 and No. 84 as the first and fourth symphonies:[1] it was no doubt part of Haydn's strategy to begin each set with a symphony of sophisticated popular appeal. In Symphony No. 87 Haydn matches the grandeur associated with C major and D major festive symphonies by employing in the exposition of the first movement a familiar grand orchestral *crescendo*, similar to the *Orchesterwalzer*, or steam-roller, generally associated with Mannheim. Whatever the origins of this specific device and however reliable its historical association with Mannheim,[2] as a grand opening to a symphony, or indeed a concerto, orchestral mannerisms associated with Mannheim were still appropriate and very much a part of popular taste in orchestral music in Paris in the

1780s. Although apart from *sforzando* accents no dynamics are indicated in the extant sources, the opening eighteen bars of Symphony No. 87/i consist of a number of textural *crescendos*, with characteristic motivic repetition and a rising tessitura. Thus, bars 4–5 repeat the music of bars 2–3 with the addition of measured violin *tremolando* in bar 4; bars 6–11 are repeated in bars 12–18, and within these larger sections bars 7–9 and 13–15 involve the insistent repetition of half-bar units, with added octave doubling, thickening of texture and rhythmic acceleration. Similar dynamic and textural effects are employed to articulate the dominant key. While there is a fairly constant *tutti, forte* texture for approximately three-quarters of the Exposition (to bar 47), the *piano* indication in the transition at bar 25 represents a dip in dynamics and textural density which prepares for the *crescendo* and rising tessitura over a dominant pedal point leading to the *forte* first theme of the dominant group (bar 37).

In employing something like a Mannheim mannerism the opening of this movement clearly appeals to a facet of popular taste which is not generally associated with Haydn symphonies.[3] Similarly, two fast *alla breve* movements in these symphonies employ opening themes of the *singende Allegro* type which, on the whole, is more associated with J. C. Bach and Mozart than with Haydn, and with the 1760s rather than the 1780s.[4] After the *Largo* introduction, the first movement of Symphony No. 84 begins with a twelve-bar lyrical melody comprising two segments in the form 8+4; an eight-bar lyrical, diatonic melody with a broken-chord accompaniment and simple harmonies stressing tonic and dominant chords; and a *forte* continuation which pauses on a half cadence on the dominant. There follows a counter-statement of ten of the previous twelve bars. The structure of the opening theme in Symphony 87/iv is in many ways similar: an eighteen-bar phrase ends with a fermata on a half cadence on the dominant leading to a counter-statement; the first phrase again comprises two segments (10+8), the first a singing diatonic melody, the second a *forte* conclusion. The comparisons between these movements extend further, in that the modulation to the dominant is effected early, and initially very simply, in both expositions; and in reaffirming the dominant at length Haydn employs a shortened and re-scored version of the opening theme in the dominant. The nature of the thematic material seems to have a far-reaching influence on both movements, in that Haydn's more characteristic motivic development is largely absent: to a considerable extent, the opening themes retain their thematic identity in development sections which favour lyrical dialogue and significant thematic restatements of the opening themes in various keys, including a false reprise in the development section of Symphony 84/i (bars 148ff.).

The other prominent aspect of popular Parisian taste strongly reflected in these symphonies is the elaborate concertante writing of the slow movements, both of which employ large-scale cadenzas, with elaborate woodwind writing, to articulate structure. In the Adagio of Symphony No. 87 the eight-bar first phrase occurs, in full or in part, six times in the movement. The counter-statement of bars 9–16 has a new counter-melody, and the reprise conflates and re-scores the initial statement and counter-statement. Elsewhere it is also re-orchestrated, so that apart from its inherent merits as a beautiful theme, very much characteristic of Haydn's mature 3/4 Adagio movements, it is a prominent vehicle for the display of orchestral colour. Flute, oboes, bassoons and horns are prominent in the orchestration of this phrase, and oboe and bassoon solos are also featured in dialogue in the lyrical second tonic theme occurring at bars 16–20 and recapitulated at bars 63–7. There is little thematic or harmonic argument in this movement; there is no discrete development section, and the melodic material is restated with decorations and changed orchestration rather than acting as a resource for the generation of new material or as the vehicle for the exercise of an elaborate tonal argument. The most prominent moments of structural articulation in this bi-partite movement are, moreover, colourful cadenzas, introduced by conventional ritornello-like passages leading to a prominent cadence on a 6-4 chord and integrating generic conventions of the concerto into the slow movement of a symphony in a way which Haydn returned to in later symphonies. Significantly, these are multi-voiced cadenzas with solos for flute and two oboes in bars 37–43 and, more elaborately, for flute, oboes, bassoons, horns and violins in bars 87–98. They bring to the symphonic tradition the woodwind concertante writing of the Parisian *symphonie concertante*. Altogether, statements and decorated or re-orchestrated restatements of the two principal melodic ideas, together with the cadenzas and their introductory ritornellos, constitute virtually the whole of this movement (the cadenzas by themselves make up nearly one-fifth of its length). It is a movement of beautiful themes and varied and colourful scoring, with vehicles for woodwind solos which might have been designed to court popular taste in Paris.

Just as the Adagio of Symphony No. 87 lacks the developmental procedures of a sonata-form movement, so too the slow movement of Symphony No. 84 largely eschews the conventional figurative variations of variation movements, emphasising instead textural and orchestral variety. Like the second movement of Symphony No. 87, it also contains a large multi-voiced cadenza. This occurs after the third variation, forming, with its introductory ritornello and concluding partial reprise of the theme of the movement, an extensive Coda. It represents the tendency, in the variation movements of the 'Paris' Symphonies and in Haydn's mature symphonic variation movements in general, to depart from the additive structure in integrative codas.[5] To this structural finesse Haydn joins a display of concertante writing which is novel and, as it were, trumps anything which even the largest solo contingent in a *symphonie concertante* might offer. The cadenza is dominated by woodwind, but from bar 74 it becomes – with the participation of the full contingent of strings (playing pizzicato*)* and with horn pedal points – a seemingly unprecedented cadenza for orchestra.[6]

Apart from the function of the Coda as peroration, this movement is in many other ways characteristic of Haydn's innovative approach to variation forms. The *minore* first variation is only loosely based on the theme, resembling it at the beginning of each phrase but developing freely and having a different phrase structure (4:‖:8 rather than 8:‖:8). Characteristically for a first variation, it also introduces dynamic and textural contrasts, reinforced by differentiation in articulation absent in the theme itself.[7] The theme and the three variations are also differentiated in scoring, with exclusively string textures and a *piano* dynamic in the theme and variation 2 contrasted with the predominantly *tutti* and *forte* scoring of variations 1 and 3. In variations 2 and 3 there is an abundance of *Setzmanieren*, the decorative figures of conventional variations, but the theme is rarely absent: indeed, much of variation 2 and all of variation 3 are *cantus firmus*-type variations, and the focus throughout is on contrasts in scoring and colour rather than virtuosic figurative writing. It is a compendium of refinements in 1780s orchestral practice, with the cadenza combining concertante wind writing and pizzicato strings being only one of its many marvels. The varied re-scoring of the melodic reprise (*a'*) of bars 13–16 at bars 41–4 and 57–60 is no less remarkable, the former an innovative duo in thirds for *bassi* and violas, the latter a remarkably rich *tutti* scoring with a new gloss on the melody scored for horns.

Neither of these movements contains the displays of thematic development or the extended harmonic vocabulary which are justly celebrated by modern commentators in Haydn's mature symphonies. Their primary attraction lies in the prodigious displays of advanced orchestral practice in structures which are adapted to, as it were, give space to popular taste. But while these symphonies conform to popular taste to an unusual degree, Haydn also retains an independence of thought; in the sonata-form movements especially, undoubtedly popular or public idioms are matched by the more *recherché* features of Haydn's mature style.

In the first instance the unity which Haydn characteristically imparts to his thematic ideas, commonly referred to as monothematicism, is witnessed in abundance but takes on a variety of forms. In the first movement of Symphony No. 87 the first theme (bars 1ff.), the theme which launches the transition at bar 19, and both of the highly contrasted themes in the dominant (bars 37ff. and 48ff.) all contain the same rhythmic head-motif. In the first movement of Symphony No. 84 (cf. bars 21–32 and 74–81) and the finale of Symphony 87 (cf. bars 1–18 and 41–57) the re-use of the first theme in the dominant is more extensive, but, typically, in each case the new version is transformed and with a different continuation from the original tonic version: in bar 74 of Symphony 84/i, for instance the scoring is for wind band rather than for strings and has a more varied texture than the homophonic *singende Allegro* version in the tonic. On the other hand, in the finale of Symphony No. 84 the unity of the principal themes in the tonic (bars 1ff.) and the dominant (bars 64ff.) is less reliant on transposed restatement; rather, melodic or rhythmic features of bars 1, 2, and 3–4 are recast in bars 64–7, 68, and 69–74 respectively, so that the dominant theme is formed from discrete developments of motifs of the first theme (see Ex. 8.1). All these movements represent very different manifestations of 'monothematicism', ranging from the sharing of a common rhythmic

Ex. 8.1a Symphony No. 84/iv, bars 1–4

Ex. 8.1b Symphony No. 84/iv, bars 64–71

head-motif, to transposed and varied restatement, to a much freer re-invention of the motivic make-up of the original theme.

These sonata-form movements also share fully in the expanded harmonic language of Haydn's mature style. In expositions this may be witnessed in elaborate transitions with more than usually complex modulations to the dominant or, where the modulation is more direct, by a compensating area of chromaticism in the dominant area. In the transition of Symphony No. 84/iv, for instance, despite the relatively secure assertion of the dominant, B♭ major, by bar 32, the following 31 bars (longer by far than the tonic area of the Exposition) contain wonderfully adventurous harmonic excursions in the minor mode, E♭ minor (IV♭/V) in bars 41–7 and B♭ minor (v) in bars 58–63, before the arrival on the 'new' theme in the dominant major key (bar 64). The transition in Symphony No. 87/i is similarly chromatic, with the dominant (E major) approached from the flat submediant (C major, bars 26–30). In contrast, the area of chromatic instability in the first movement of Symphony No. 84 occurs after the clear articulation of the dominant: here, after a single phrase in B♭ major (bars 74–80), for twelve bars Haydn employs a digression, much favoured in his works from the 1780s, to the dominant minor key and flat submediant of the dominant, before restoring B♭ major. In all of these expositions Haydn's harmonic vocabulary is just as rich and the definition of the dominant key just as complex as in others of the 'Paris' Symphonies, whether in chromatic transitions or areas of harmonic instability in the second half of the exposition.

Development sections in the first and fourth movements of Symphony No. 84 begin in the dominant in a manner more akin to symphonies of the 1760s than to Haydn's fondness, especially in his later works, for harmonic surprises at this point of the movement; commencing the Development of Symphony 87/i in the tonic minor is scarcely more adventurous. None the less, the extent of these development sections and their harmonic range as a whole are characteristic of the enhanced importance and expanded chromatic language of development sections in Haydn's 1780s symphonies. In scale alone these development sections are extensive (30% of the entire movement in 87/i, 36% in 84/i and iv, and, remarkably, 50% in 87/iv where the Recapitulation is reduced to a mere 21 bars, one-quarter of the length of the Exposition). They are equally lavish in the range of their harmonic argument, particularly in the first movement of Symphony No. 87, in which the point of furthest tonal remove from the tonic (A major) is the prolonged G♯ major⁷ (V/iii). Equally remarkably, the return to the tonic involves an elision by which V/iii is followed by an abrupt mediant shift to V. The effect of these radical harmonies is enhanced by the static nature of the theme which articulates the progressions, by the abrupt manner of arriving at V⁷/iii (a tonal shift from vi at bars 112–13) and by the two bars of silence which separate the mediant juxtaposition V/iii–V (bars 122–5). In the finale of Symphony No. 84 a mediant relationship is employed to articulate a false reprise at bar 118 (V⁷/ii–IV), and the false reprise in the supertonic at bar 148 of the first movement is prepared by a chromatic rising bass, similar to the chromatic bass employed in the retransition (bars 181–8). The retransition of Symphony 84/iv is no less extraordinary in its emphasis on the minor tonic and subdominant (bars 156–89) elaborating on the parallel chromatic interruption in the dominant area of the Exposition (cf. bars 44–62).

At various points in these movements, therefore, it is clear that the language of Haydn's popular style is fully contemporary, employing an extended harmonic vocabulary in sophisticated transitions, chromatic instability in the dominant tonal area of the expositions, and extensive development sections in terms of their length and harmonic range. By comparison with other 'Paris' Symphonies, notably No. 82 and 85, the recapitulations in the sonata-form movements of Symphonies No. 84 and 87 are concise and contain relatively few new features by comparison with expositions. However, in the first movement of Symphony No. 87, perhaps compensating for the relatively short Development section (62 bars as against 91 in Symphony 84/i, 106 bars in 84/iv, and 108 bars in 87/iv), the extensively recomposed Recapitulation and a process of developing variation throughout the movement are equal in sophistication to anything found elsewhere in the 'Paris' Symphonies. The significant new developments in the Recapitulation occur in connection with the first theme and the transition:

Exposition		*Recapitulation*	
Theme 1	1–18		131–44
			145–52
		Theme 2	153–6
Transition/Theme 2	19–36		157–70

In this Recapitulation the statement of the first theme is shortened by four bars in comparison with the Exposition, but an entirely new continuation employs a motif from the first theme as a point of imitation in a way which occurs nowhere else in the movement. The beginning of the second theme, which launches the transition in the Exposition, is also radically rewritten in the Recapitulation, with new melodic figures and a completely transformed and enriched texture (bars 153–6). These are new developments in comparison with an original transition which is itself notable for a subtle process of developing variation (see Ex. 8.2). As mentioned above, the head-motif of the transition (up-beat to bar 19) is derived from the first theme: after bar 19 its melodic identity as a repeated-note figure (x) is lost, but its rhythmic identity is retained (x') through to bar 22, after which the focus of attention is switched to the new motif y, which is transformed from the *sforzando* disjunct motif in minims to a *sforzando* conjunct motif (y') and finally to a *legato* and *piano* conjunct motif (y''). In this process of incremental change y'' bears little kinship to y except through y'. Motifs x, y' and y'' subsequently become the basis for much of the development section (especially bars 84–100), and the x motif is further transformed, as mentioned above, in bars 152–4 of the recapitulation.

The minuets of Symphonies Nos. 84 and 87 lack the scale for elaborate tonal argument of the type mentioned above in connection with sonata-form movements. In Symphony No. 84, the second, 'modulatory', phrase is entirely set over a dominant pedal; and that in Symphony No. 87/iii, while twice as long, is scarcely more elaborate harmonically,

Ex. 8.2 Symphony No. 87/i, bars 19–26

remaining strongly focused on the dominant (bars 13–20) and the minor tonic (bars 21–4). Neither is the thematic elaboration in the second phrase of the minuets particularly elaborate, and indeed in the second phrase of Symphony No. 84/iii it is confined to conventional phrase extensions, a threefold reiteration of the half cadence on the dominant of bars 15–16. The main focus of attention in these minuets is, rather, on textural, orchestral and dynamic variety after impressive *tutti* and *forte* first phrases.

The first phrases of both minuets are alike in orchestration and texture and in their regularity of phrase structure (4+4+4 in No. 84/iii and 4+4 in No. 87/iii), and, in comparison, the primary novelty in the second halves of the minuets is their more diversifed textures. This is true of the second phrases (for instance, the changing orchestration in the cadence repetition of bars 15–20 in Symphony No. 84/iii) and particularly the reprises and codettas. In Symphony No. 84/iii the reprise contains textural contrasts lacking in the first phrase, in that the reinforced scoring of the first six bars is contrasted with the thinner texture and *piano* dynamic of the new six-bar parenthetical interpolation (bars 27–32). In Symphony No. 87/iii the reprise (bars 25–32) is an unvaried restatement of the first phrase, but it is followed by a typically extensive Coda (4+4+6+6 as opposed to 4+4), which develops the cadence figure of the first phrase and has a faster rate of textural change than anywhere else in the movement (two bars of first violins and horns + four bars *tutti*, both repeated with alterations).

Against this characteristic orchestral brilliance and colour the Trio of Symphony No. 87 is entirely different in its appeal. Unlike the minuets, it is unvaried in texture, and the reprise of the first phrase is literal. However, the continuous lyrical oboe solo, with only a sparse string accompaniment, confined harmonically in the first and third phrases to tonic and dominant chords, is the quintessential 'beautiful' melody. While appealing, like the trios of Symphonies Nos. 85 and 86, to the French *penchant* for woodwind solos, it represents at the same time a Rousseauian ideal for natural instrumental music, which reminds us why eighteenth-century Parisian audiences found Haydn's music remarkable for its melodic grace as well as orchestral splendour and compositional sophistication. The minuets and trios of Symphonies Nos. 84 and 87 contain within their limited horizons as much finesse and contrast as their companion movements, and Haydn's wish that something entirely new be accomplished in the minuet is reflected in a wealth of sophisticated detail.

It is not possible to document that Haydn had a detailed knowledge of the musical taste of his Parisian public, and it is certainly true that he had no first-hand experience of this audience as he had at Eszterháza and was later concerned to acquire in London. As suggested elsewhere in this study, the reconciliation of popular and learned taste which is characteristic of Haydn's symphonies provided a basis for his popular appeal even without the opportunity for the specific appraisal of his audience. In Symphonies Nos. 84 and 87 Haydn goes further than in other 'Paris' Symphonies towards courting popular taste, the expectation of a public accustomed to large orchestras, virtuosos of all instruments, and an orchestral palette informed by two generations of Mannheim symphonists. Yet Haydn's popular style is enriched by the same sophisticated compositional technique as the more *recherché* Symphony No. 85. Symphonies Nos. 84 and 87 represent a refined and up-dated popular style in much the same way as the slightly later Trios, Hob. XV:15–16 (1790), re-invent an earlier galant style in Haydn's musical language of the late 1780s. Although they strike a different balance between originality and popularity than in Symphonies Nos. 83 and 85, Symphonies Nos. 84 and 87 are equally representative of Haydn's judgement of musical taste, his desire that 'nothing [be] overdone'. This compositional propriety, which is acknowledged in contemporary writings, is also central to Rosen's characterisation of Haydn's mature symphonies as 'heroic pastoral' and to the understanding of Haydn's style as Classical, in the sense of a con-trolled, mature language at home in its time.

Notes

1 Introduction

1 The autograph manuscripts of Symphonies Nos. 83 and 87 are dated 1785; those of Symphonies Nos. 82, 84 and 86, 1786. The autograph fragment of Symphony No. 85 is undated.

2 M. Brenet, *Les Concerts en France sous l'ancien régime* (Paris, 1900; repr., New York: Da Capo, 1970), p. 366. See also F.-J. Fétis, *Curiosités historiques de la musique* (Paris, 1830), p. 333, quoted in *Joseph Haydn Werke*, I,12 (Munich: Henle, 1971), p. vi.

3 Quoted in J.-L. Quoy-Bodin, 'L'Orchestre de la Société Olympique en 1786', *Revue de musicologie* 70 (1984): 96. On the Comte d'Ogny and the *Concert de la Loge Olympique* see esp. Brenet, *Les Concerts en France*, pp. 363–6; B. Brook, *La Symphonie française dans la seconde moitié du XVIIIe siècle* (Paris: Institut de Musicologie de l'Université de Paris, 1962), vol. 1, pp. 340–9; H. C. R. Landon, *Haydn: Chronicle and Works*, vol. 2, *Haydn at Eszterháza, 1766–1790* (London: Thames & Hudson, 1978), pp. 590–4.

4 Landon, *Haydn at Eszterháza*, p. 594.

5 *Mercure de France*, 26 Jan. 1788, p. 192. The announcement is quoted in full in Chapter 2.

6 Letters of 26 April and 2 May 1787. H. C. R. Landon, ed., *The Collected Correspondence and London Notebooks of Joseph Haydn* (London: Barrie & Rockliff, 1959), pp. 61–2 (hereafter cited as *CCLN*). Although Artaria was initially offered pirated copies of the symphonies indirectly, it is clear that their print was an authentic edition, approved and proofread by Haydn. With a letter of 22 Nov. 1787 Haydn returned 'the corrected Quartets and Symphonies', i.e. the string quartets Op. 50 and Symphonies Nos. 82–7.

7 *CCLN*, p. 69.

8 *Ibid.*, p. 70.

9 *Ibid.*, p. 61. See also the letter to Artaria of 19 May 1787 (*ibid.*, p. 63).

10 See W. D. Sutcliffe, *Haydn: String Quartets, Op. 50*, Cambridge Music Handbooks (Cambridge: Cambridge University Press, 1992), pp. 33–6.

11 According to the title pages the string quartet arrangements are by the composer, although there is no extant documentation to corroborate the claim. Sieber's later arrangements, possibly derived from the Artaria edition, make the same claim.

12 This particularly skilful and idiomatic arrangement of Symphony No. 82 was prepared by Clementi.

13 The keyboard arrangement of Symphony No. 82 by Steegman which appeared in the *Harmonicon* in 1829 bore the subtitle 'Le Danse de l'Ours', which is, as far as I can establish, the first use of this nickname in connection with the symphony. I have located no eighteenth-century source for the nickname 'La Poule' for Symphony No. 83, and thus 'La Reine', the name given to Symphony No. 85 in the Imbault edition, appears to be the only one derived from eighteenth-century usage.

14 RISM no. H3135. Later re-issues by Forster [*c*.1815] mention performances at the 'Professional and other Public Concerts', e.g. Symphonies Nos. 82 and 84, British Library copies h.656.l.(10) and h.656.l.(13).

15 See N. Zaslaw, *Mozart's Symphonies: Context, Performance Practice, Reception* (Oxford: Oxford University Press, 1989), p. 459. Cf. Brook, *La Symphonie française*, vol. 1, pp. 328, 332, 336.

16 See Quoy-Bodin, 'L'Orchestre de la Société Olympique en 1786', pp. 100–4. Landon's claim that the orchestra of the *Concert de la Loge Olympique* had 'forty violins and ten double-basses' (*Haydn at Eszterháza*, p. 593, and repeated elsewhere) appears to derive from Brenet's statement about the orchestra of the *Concert des amateurs* (Brenet, *Les Concerts en France*, pp. 360–1). It misrepresents the balance in the orchestras of the *Concert spirituel* and the *Concert de la Loge Olympique*.

2 Haydn's music and the Concert spirituel

1 J. H. Johnson, *Listening in Paris: A Cultural History* (Berkeley: University of California Press, 1995), pp. 197–205. See also *idem*, 'Beethoven and the Birth of Romantic Musical Experience in France', *19th-Century Music* 15 (1991): 23–35, esp. 29–30.

2 The programmes of the *Concert spirituel* are established in A. Bloch-Michel's 'Programmes du Concert Spirituel' in C. Pierre, *Histoire du Concert spirituel, 1725–1790* (Paris: Société Française de Musicologie, 1975), pp. 229–344. The statistics used in this chapter, compiled with the help of Bloch-Michel's listings, should be regarded as approximations. That they do not in all respects agree with statistics in Pierre's text is due to different methods of calculation and to some errors and omissions which I have rectified.

References to particular concerts, as opposed to global statistics, are generally drawn directly from accounts in the Parisian press rather than from
Pierre.

3 In some accounts of the programme for 7 April 1773 the performance of a
Haydn symphony is mentioned. See Bloch-Michel/Pierre, *Histoire du
Concert spirituel*, p. 301.

4 On the catalogue of the Comte d'Ogny see in particular B. Brook, *La Symphonie française*, pp. 341–9.

5 Gossec, Le Gros's predecessor as director of the *Concert spirituel*, had from
1769 to 1773 been a director of the *Concert des amateurs*. See Brenet, *Les Concerts en France*, pp. 299–302, 309–10, 357–630.

6 Bloch-Michel/Pierre, *Histoire du Concert spirituel*, p. 306.

7 Landon, *The Symphonies of Joseph Haydn* (London: Universal & Rockliff,
1955), p. 701. It might well be the case that Haydn's Symphony No. 56 was
the work performed in the *Concert spirituel* of 25 March 1777, since the work
performed on this occasion was 'au répertoire des Amateurs'; the d'Ogny
catalogue suggests that Symphony No. 56 was in the repertoire of the *Concert
des amateurs*, while the Sieber print identifies the same symphony with both
the *Concert des amateurs* and the *Concert spirituel*.

8 Brenet, *Les Concerts en France*, pp. 221–4.

9 *Mercure de France*, 21 August 1779, pp. 136–7.

10 Brook, *La Symphonie française*, vol. 1, pp. 259, 350.

11 *Ibid.*, pp. 145–67; Brenet, *Les Concerts en France*, pp. 224–6, 267–8, 301–10.

12 Brook, *La Symphonie française*, vol. 1, pp. 160–1, 166.

13 Brenet, *Les Concerts en France*, p. 267.

14 See in particular Zaslaw, *Mozart's Symphonies*, pp. 309ff.; *idem*, 'Mozart's
Paris Symphonies', *Musical Times* 119 (1978): 753–7.

15 Letter of 3 July 1778. E. Anderson, ed., *The Letters of Mozart and His Family*,
2nd edn (London: Macmillan, 1966), vol. 2, pp. 556–9.

16 Zaslaw lists the 15 performances of Mozart symphonies in 'Mozart's Paris
Symphonies', pp. 755–6. To this list of performances of Mozart symphonies
at the *Concert spirituel* one should add the performance by Melle Willieaume of
a Mozart concerto on the 'forté-piano' in the concert of 10 April 1786 (see
Annonces, affiches & avis divers, 10 April 1786) and the performance of a
Mozart aria in the *Concert spirituel* of 21 April 1778 (cited in Bloch-
Michel/Pierre, *Histoire du Concert spirituel*, p. 309).

17 *Mercure de France*, 5 June 1779, p. 48.

18 *Mercure de France*, April 1778, vol. 2, p. 163, reporting on the concert of 25
March 1778.

19 *Mercure de France*, 5 Jan. 1779, p. 46; 15 April 1779, p. 179.

20 *Mercure de France*, 25 May 1779, p. 291. See also *Mercure de France*, 21 Dec. 1782. Similarly, as late as 1784, in a long review of Haydn's 'Farewell' Symphony, the reviewer is approving of the spectacle and of the 'sad and lugubrious melody' of the closing 'Andante' [*recte* Adagio] but dismisses the preceding Presto as 'a noisy piece and without character' (*Mercure de France*, 24 April 1784, pp. 180–1). Appropriately enough, this symphony was chosen by Le Gros for the final *Concert spirituel* to be held in the Salle des Suisses of the Château des Tuileries before the series moved to the Salle des Machines.

21 *Mercure de France*, 15 Sept. 1779, p. 118, quoted in Landon, *Symphonies*, p. 375.

22 *Mercure de France*, 6 Nov. 1779, p. 32.

23 *CCLN*, p. 28.

24 *Mercure de France*, 21 April 1781, p. 129.

25 See in particular R. Isherwood, 'The Third War of the Musical Enlightenment', *Studies in Eighteenth-Century Culture* 4, ed. H. Pagliaro (Madison: University of Wisconsin Press, 1975), pp. 223–45; E. Lowinsky, 'Taste, Style, and Ideology in Eighteenth-Century Music', in *Aspects of the Eighteenth Century*, ed. E. Wasserman (Baltimore: Johns Hopkins University Press, 1965), pp. 163–205.

26 See Pierre, *Histoire du Concert spirituel*, pp. 108, 221–2, and *passim*.

27 This calculation is marginally different from that in Pierre, *Histoire du Concert spirituel*, pp. 221–2.

28 *Mercure de France*, 21 April 1781, pp. 129–30.

29 *Mercure de France*, 16 April 1785, p. 125.

30 See Pierre, *Histoire de Concert spirituel*, pp. 176–7, 179.

31 *Mercure de France*, 21 April 1781, p. 129.

32 'The two Stabat[s] were again performed, and both were very deeply felt and applauded' (*Mercure de France*, 28 April 1781, p. 185).

33 *Ibid.*, pp. 185–6.

34 'One heard with new pleasure the Stabat of Hayden and that of Pergolèze' (*Mercure de France*, 20 April 1782, p. 131); 'The concert was interspersed with fragments of the Stabat of M. Hayden, which merit still new praises' (*Mercure de France*, 15 Nov. 1783, p. 133); 'We will not speak at all of the Stabat of M. Hayden, which had its accustomed success' (*Mercure de France*, 29 April 1786, p. 245).

35 See for instance the reviews in the *Mercure de France* of 21 April 1781, pp. 129–31; 28 April 1781, pp. 185–6; 20 April 1782, pp. 131–2; 29 April 1786, p. 245; 28 April 1787, p. 175.

36 'If the Stabat of Pergolèze is so beautiful, it is above all because it is simple, because one idea and the developments of the same idea suffice for each

verset. M. Hayden, who in his Stabat did not follow the same course as Pergolèze, approached it on this point' (*Mercure de France*, 10 May 1783, p. 82).

37 *Mercure de France*, 28 June 1783, pp. 193–4.

38 See *Mercure de France*, 6 May 1786, pp. 38–9. In this lengthy review the composer is erroneously given as M. David, who was in fact one of the soloists in the performance.

39 See *Mercure de France*, 28 April 1787, p. 175, and 12 April 1788, p. 81. See also Pierre, *Histoire du Concert spirituel*, p. 179.

40 *Mercure de France*, 16 Nov. 1782, p. 137.

41 *Mercure de France*, 17 Sept. 1785, p. 139.

42 *Mercure de France*, 11 Nov. 1786, p. 92.

43 *Mercure de France*, 17 Feb. 1787, pp. 127–8.

44 *Mercure de France*, 20 Sept. 1783, p. 135.

45 I. Kant, *Kritik der Urtheilskraft* (Berlin, 1790), part 1, book 2, § 46; trans. W. S. Pluhar (Indianapolis: Hackett, 1987), pp. 174–5.

46 *Ibid.*, trans. Pluhar, p. 175.

47 *Mercure de France*, 7 April 1787, pp. 32–3.

48 G. A. Griesinger, *Biographische Notizen über Joseph Haydn*, trans. V. Gotwals in *Joseph Haydn: Eighteenth-Century Gentleman and Genius* (Madison: University of Wisconsin Press, 1963), pp. 60–1.

49 Occasionally the two symphonies were placed as the first and last items of the concert.

50 See the review in the *Mercure de France*, 5 June 1779, p. 48, quoted above.

51 From 1788 to 1790 two symphonies by Haydn were performed in 54% of concerts. In five further concerts a Haydn symphony and his Stabat Mater (or part of it) were performed; one of these concerts also contained excerpts from *The Seven Last Words*.

52 *Mercure de France*, 26 Jan. 1788, p. 192.

53 See for instance the advertisements in the *Mercure de France* of 8 March 1788, p. 96; 10 May 1788, p. 96; 22 Nov. 1788, p. 191.

54 *Mercure de France*, 12 April 1788, pp. 77–8.

55 Landon, *Symphonies*, p. 401. See also *idem*, *Haydn at Eszterháza*, p. 593.

56 The word 'presque' is lacking here in Landon's quotation. The date of the review is also incorrectly given as 5 April 1788.

57 C. Rosen, *Sonata Forms* (New York: Norton, 1980), p. 5.

58 'Quoique les Concerts de cette quinzaine aient présenté au Public très peu de nouveautés, ils n'ont pas laissé que d'être fort suivis' (*Mercure de France*, 12 April 1788, p. 77).

59 Bloch-Michel/Pierre suggests that the review covers the concerts of 22 to 31 March (*Histoire du Concert spirituel*, p. 339), but a number of the per-

formances mentioned refer to concerts before 22 March and as early as 9 March. For instance, the ode by l'abbé Dedieu mentioned in the review was performed in the concerts of the 9 and 10 March, and the *clavecin* concerto performed by Mlle Moulinghem was in the concert of 9 March. (Cf. *Mercure de France*, 12 April 1788, pp. 78–9, and Bloch-Michel/Pierre, *Histoire du Concert spirituel*, pp. 337–9).

60 See for instance the title pages of the Sieber edition and the Boyer arrangements, given in A. van Hoboken, *Joseph Haydn: Thematisch-bibliographisches Werkverzeichnis* (Mainz: Schott, 1957–78), vol. 1, pp. 142–3, 148.

61 A Haydn symphony or symphonies 'en ut' performed on a number of occasions in 1790 might well have been Symphony No. 82, although Symphony No. 90, from the later Paris set and available in Paris in 1790, is also a possible candidate.

62 Cf. Bloch-Michel/Pierre, *Histoire du Concert spirituel*, pp. 343–4, and Hoboken, *Werkverzeichnis*, vol. 1, pp. 158ff.

63 See for instance Landon, *Symphonies*, pp. 435–593, and *idem*, *Haydn: Chronicle and Works*, vol. 3, *Haydn in England* (London: Thames & Hudson, 1976).

64 See Johnson, *Listening in Paris*, p. 202. See also *idem*, 'Beethoven and the Birth of Romantic Musical Experience in France', pp. 23–35, esp. 29–30.

65 *The Monthly Musical Magazine and Review* 2 (1820): 283.

3 Popular taste

1 The important vocal repertoire of the *Concert spirituel* and the long tradition of presenting regularly the leading European singers lie outside the scope of the present study. See Pierre, *Histoire du Concert spirituel*, and Brenet, *Les Concerts en France, passim*.

2 The clarinettist listed by Quoy-Bodin as a member of the orchestra of the Société Olympique in 1786 may safely be identified as Michel Yost. See Quoy-Bodin, 'L'Orchestre de la Société Olympique en 1786', p. 103.

3 *Mercure de France*, 29 April 1786, p. 242.

4 *Annonces, affiches & avis divers*, 16 April 1786, p. 991.

5 In 1778, for instance, the oboist Ramm, the flautist Wendling, the singers Dorothea Wendling and Anton Raaf, and Anton Stamitz were all in Paris and appeared at the *Concert spirituel*. The second-generation Mannheim oboist Ludwig August Lebrun dominated the concerto repertoire in the 1777 and 1779 seasons, making at least 23 appearances in these two years.

6 See P.-L. Ginguené, 'Concerto', in *Encyclopédie méthodique*, quoted in J. Mongrédien, 'Paris: The End of the Ancien Régime', in *Man & Music: The Classical Era*, ed. N. Zaslaw (London: Macmillan, 1989), p. 77.

7 On the clarinet virtuosos of the *Concert spirituel*, see Pierre, *Histoire du Concert spirituel*, pp. 214–15. Notwithstanding the relatively early introduction of the fortepiano into the *Concert spirituel* in 1768 (see Brenet, *Les Concerts en France*, pp. 292–3), the instrument was not accepted uncritically in Paris, and it does not appear with any frequency in *Concert spirituel* programmes until after the mid 1780s (see my *Haydn's Keyboard Music: Studies in Performance Practice* (Oxford: Clarendon Press, 1997), p. 2). The piano concerto repertoire of the *Concert spirituel* was also, it must be said, fairly impoverished by comparison with the 1780s Viennese repertoire. The performance of a Mozart piano concerto by Melle Willieaume (advertised *Annonces, affiches & avis divers*, 10 April 1786) was exceptional; and the performance, on a 'forté-piano organisé', of a Clementi concerto by Melle Candeille on 15 Aug. 1783 (mentioned in *Mercure de France*, 23 August 1783, p. 188) is of interest because no concerto by Clementi is known to be extant.

8 Brook, *La Symphonie française*, vol. 1, pp. 350, 468, 474.

9 *Ibid.*, p. 468.

10 *Mercure de France*, 16 April 1785, p. 120.

11 See W. Weber, 'Learned and General Musical Taste in Eighteenth-Century France', *Past and Present* 89 (1980): 58–85.

12 Hob. XVIII:4 was performed by Maria Theresia Paradies in April 1784 (see H. Walter, ed., *Joseph Haydn: Konzerte für Klavier (Cembalo) und Orchester*, JHW, XV,2 (Munich: Henle, 1983), p. vi). A Haydn fortepiano concerto was performed by Mlle Landrin on 26 March 1785 and probably again on 8 Sept. 1785 (see Pierre, *Histoire du Concert spirituel*, pp. 329–30).

13 See Quoy-Bodin, 'L'Orchestre de la Société Olympique en 1786', pp. 95–107.

14 *Mercure de France*, 14 Feb. 1784, p. 81.

15 *Mercure de France*, 26 March 1785, p. 179.

16 Cited after the advertisements in *Annonces, affiches, & avis divers*, 22 April 1786 and 13 August 1786.

17 The symphony or symphonies with obbligatos for horns and oboes were performed on 8 Dec. 1784, 4 April 1785, 23 April 1786, 15 Aug. 1786, 1 April 1787, 25 Dec. 1789, and 9 April 1790. The symphony advertised as having horn obbligatos was performed on 5 April 1787.

18 It was published jointly by Sieber and Imbault under the title 'Simphonie périodique' in 1784. Although it is beyond the scope of the present discussion, there appears to be a strong connection between the repertoire of the *Concert spirituel* and the Sieber publications, particularly those called 'Simphonies périodiques'.

19 See Brenet, *Les Concerts en France*, pp. 222–7, and Brook, *La Symphonie française*, vol. 1, p. 163.

20 Cited after *Annonces, affiches, & avis divers*, 7 April 1786. The soloists are listed in *Journal de Paris*, 11 April 1786, p. 412.

21 'Nouvelle Symphonie concertante de M. Haydn, violon, violoncelle, flûtes, hautbois, cors et contre basse obligés' (*Annonces, affiches, & avis divers*, 11 April 1786).

22 *Mercure de France*, 29 April 1786, p. 243.

23 *Mercure de France*, 20 Sept. 1788, p. 144. See also Hoboken, *Werkverzeichnis*, vol. 1, p. 246; Landon, *Symphonies*, p. 809. The edition is RISM no. H3278.

24 Another print of the 'Hornsignal' from Forster (RISM no. H3052) also has the title 'A concertante sinfonia'. Apart from the 'Hornsignal', other Haydn symphonies appeared in eighteenth-century editions with the title *symphonie concertante* or its equivalent: e.g. No. 13 in a Silly print (H3047); and No. 63 (H3092), No. 72 (H2784) and No. 87 (H2756) in English prints by Forster and Bland.

25 See Brook, *La Symphonie française*, vol. 1, pp. 84–93, 179–89.

26 Mozart, letter of 3 July 1778 (Anderson, ed., *Letters*, vol. 2, p. 558). Leopold Mozart commented rather sceptically on this aspect of Parisian taste in a letter of 29 June 1778: 'To judge by the Stamitz symphonies which have been engraved in Paris, the Parisians must be fond of noisy music. For these are nothing but noise. Apart from this they are a hodge-podge, with here and there a good idea, but introduced awkwardly and in quite the wrong place' (*ibid.*, p. 556).

27 Many of these symphonies were published in Paris in the late 1770s and in the 1780s, including Symphony No. 48 ('Maria Theresia'), which was made available *c*.1784 in an Imbault print; two C major symphonies (Nos. 56 and 63) were performed at the *Concert spirituel* according to the title pages of the Boyer and Sieber editions, the former also having strong associations with the *Concert des amateurs*; and a symphony or symphonies in C major were performed twice at the *Concert spirituel* in April 1790.

4 Learned taste

1 Voltaire, *Candide,* trans. J. Butt (London: Penguin, 1947), p. 119.

2 Batteux, *Les Beaux-arts réduits à un même principe* (Paris, 1746); partial trans. in P. Le Huray and J. Day, *Music and Aesthetics in the Eighteenth and Early-Nineteenth Centuries,* abridged edn (Cambridge: Cambridge University Press, 1988), pp. 32–47.

3 Kant, *Kritik der Urtheilskraft*, part 1, book 2, §44, trans. Pluhar, pp. 172–3.

4 Concerning the aesthetics of instrumental music see, in particular, J. Neubauer, *The Emancipation of Music from Language: Departures from Mimesis in Eighteenth-Century Aesthetics* (New Haven: Yale University Press, 1986).

5 Rousseau, *Dictionnaire de musique* (Geneva, 1767), s. v. 'Unité de mélodie'; trans. in Le Huray and Day, *Music and Aesthetics*, p. 93.

6 Rousseau, *Essai sur l'origine des langues*, trans. in E. Fubini, *Music and Culture in Eighteenth-Century Europe: A Source Book*, ed. B. Blackburn (Chicago: University of Chicago Press, 1994), p. 97.

7 See P. Gay, *The Enlightenment: An Interpretation*, 2 vols. (New York: Vintage, 1966, 1969).

8 See D. G. Charlton, *New Images of the Natural in France: A Study in European Cultural History, 1750–1800* (Cambridge: Cambridge University Press, 1984); L. Jordanova, ed., *Languages of Nature: Critical Essays on Science and Literature* (London: Free Association Books, 1986).

9 Rousseau, *Dictionnaire de musique*, s.v. 'Naturel'; trans. in Le Huray and Day, *Music and Aesthetics*, p. 89.

10 For informed discussions see Neubauer, *The Emancipation of Music from Language*; E. Fubini, *History of Music Aesthetics*, trans. M. Hatwell (London: Macmillan, 1990); E. Lippman, *A History of Western Musical Aesthetics* (Lincoln: University of Nebraska Press, 1992); C. Verba, *Music and the French Enlightenment: Reconstruction of a Dialogue 1750–1764* (Oxford: Oxford University Press, 1993); Isherwood, 'The Third War of the Musical Enlightenment'; Lowinsky, 'Taste, Style, and Ideology in Eighteenth-Century Music'; D. Launay, ed., *La Querelle des Bouffons: Texte des pamphlets avec introduction, commentaires, et index*, 3 vols. (Geneva: Minkoff, 1973).

11 See Isherwood, 'The Third War of the Musical Enlightenment', esp. pp. 227ff.

12 Gluck, Preface to *Alceste*, trans. in Fubini, *Music and Culture*, p. 365.

13 Gluck, 'Lettre de M. le Chevalier Gluck, sur la musique', *Mercure de France*, Feb. 1773, p. 182; trans. in Le Huray and Day, *Music and Aesthetics*, p. 116.

14 Guy de Chabanon, *Observations on Music and Principally on the Metaphysics of Art*, trans. in Fubini, *Music and Culture*, pp. 379–80, 382–3.

15 See Weber, 'Learned and General Musical Taste in Eighteenth-Century France'.

16 *Mercure de France,* 5 Jan. 1779, pp. 46–7.

17 *Mercure de France,* 1 Jan. 1780, pp. 33–4.

18 *Mercure de France,* 15 April 1786, p. 159.

19 *Mercure de France,* 1 Jan. 1780, p. 35.

20 Mongrédien, 'Paris: The End of the Ancien Régime', p. 63.

21 *Ibid.* For similar attitudes to the relationship between aesthetics and instrumental music in the eighteenth century see Brook, *La Symphonie française*, vol. 1, pp. 333–6.

22 *Mercure de France*, 7 April 1781, p. 33.

23 *CCLN*, p. 8. The Stabat Mater and the testimonial from Hasse received special mention in Haydn's autobiographical sketch of 1776 (*CCLN*, p. 20).

24 *Mercure de France*, 29 April 1786, p. 244.

25 *Mercure de France*, 28 April 1787, p. 172.

26 D. Schroeder, *Haydn and the Enlightenment: The Late Symphonies and Their Audience* (Oxford: Clarendon, 1990), p. 67.

27 C. Dahlhaus, *Foundations of Music History*, trans. J. B. Robinson (Cambridge: Cambridge University Press, 1983), pp. 33–43.

28 J. La Rue, 'Symphony', in *The New Grove Dictionary of Music and Musicians*, ed. S. Sadie (London: Macmillan, 1980).

29 J. Webster, 'When Did Haydn Begin to Write "Beautiful" Melodies?' in *Haydn Studies: Proceedings of the International Haydn Conference, Washington, D.C., 1975*, ed. J. P. Larsen, H. Serwer, J. Webster (New York: Norton, 1981), pp. 385–8.

30 Schroeder, *Haydn and the Enlightenment*, p. 68.

5 Splendour and beauty: Symphonies Nos. 82 and 86

1 J. A. P. Schulz, 'Symphonie', in J. G. Sulzer, *Allgemeine Theorie der schönen Künste* (Leipzig, 1771–4; facsimile of 2nd edn, Hildesheim: Olms, 1994), vol. 4, pp. 478–9.

2 See E. R. Sisman, *Mozart: The 'Jupiter' Symphony*, Cambridge Music Handbooks (Cambridge: Cambridge University Press, 1993), pp. 9–15.

3 See R. Steblin, *History of Key Characteristics in the Eighteenth and Early Nineteenth Centuries* (Ann Arbor: UMI, 1983).

4 Apart from symphonies, C major is associated with festive masses featuring prominent trumpet and drum parts, and with other genres. Mozart's C major Piano Concerto, K. 503, for instance, displays many of the characteristics of festive C major music.

5 See especially Sisman, *'Jupiter' Symphony*, and J. de Ruiter, *Der Charakterbegriff in der Musik: Studien zur deutschen Ästhetik der Instrumentalmusik, 1740–1850*, Beihefte zum Archiv für Musikwissenschaft, 29 (Stuttgart: Steiner, 1989), pp. 175–204.

6 See Sisman, *'Jupiter' Symphony*, pp. 47–8 on the similarities between this opening and that in Mozart's 'Paris' Symphony, K. 297. Sisman sees the continuation of bars 5–8 as a contrast in *topos*, evocative of a minuet. The

generic associations of these bars seem to me less significant than the aesthetic connotations discussed below.

7 *Ibid.*, p. 48.

8 See C. Dahlhaus, 'What is Developing Variation?' in *Schoenberg and the New Music*, trans. D. Puffett and A. Clayton (Cambridge: Cambridge University Press, 1987), pp. 128–33; D. Epstein, *Beyond Orpheus: Studies in Musical Structure* (Oxford: Oxford University Press, 1987), pp. 3–21; J. Webster, *Haydn's 'Farewell' Symphony and the Idea of Classical Style* (Cambridge: Cambridge University Press, 1991), pp. 194–204.

9 C. G. Körner, 'Über Charakterdarstellung in der Musik', trans. in Le Huray and Day, *Music and Aesthetics*, p. 177. On Körner's text see de Ruiter, *Charakterbegriff*, pp. 127–58.

10 Rosen, *Sonata Forms*, p. 5.

11 See Webster, 'When did Haydn Begin to Write "Beautiful Melodies"?' p. 388; Schroeder, *Haydn and the Enlightenment*, pp. 78–82.

12 This closing theme has certain similarities to bars 1–8 in the way the two *forte* chords and rests of bars 86 and 91 are followed by a *piano* and more lyrical cadence figure (cf. bars 4–5).

13 On this aspect of Haydn's sonata style see especially Webster, *Haydn's 'Farewell' Symphony*, pp. 165–73; E. K. Wolf, 'The Recapitulations in Haydn's London Symphonies', *Musical Quarterly* 52 (1966): 71–89.

14 The status of this theme is problematic in relation to sonata-form theory, and such themes have been described by Dahlhaus as an 'interpolated episode, which lacks a name' (C. Dahlhaus, *Ludwig van Beethoven: Approaches to His Music*, trans. M. Whittall (Oxford: Clarendon Press, 1991), p. 102). In bars 60ff. of Symphony No. 82/i this impression is given by the dominant pedal point and by the imitative and chromatic nature of the theme itself. Although in the dominant, it represents a weak articulation of the dominant by comparison with the main thematic contrast of bars 70ff.

15 Schulz, 'Symphonie', in Sulzer, *Allgemeine Theorie*, vol. 4, p. 479.

16 Webster, 'When did Haydn Begin to Write "Beautiful Melodies"?' p. 388.

17 Cf. the first variation of Symphony No. 85/ii and the first (*minore*) variation of Symphony No. 84/ii.

18 On this characteristic of Haydn's variation movements see E. Sisman, 'Haydn's Hybrid Variations', in *Haydn Studies*, ed. J. P. Larsen *et al.* pp. 511–12.

19 This phrase also contains cross-beat and cross-bar articulation which contrasts strongly with the articulation in the rest of the movement. On Haydn's use of articulation as variation see my *Haydn's Keyboard Music: Studies in Performance Practice*, pp. 69–84.

20 See L. Ratner, *Classic Music: Expression, Form, and Style* (New York: Schirmer, 1980), p. 21, and H. C. Koch, *Musikalisches Lexikon* (Frankfurt, 1802; facsimile repr., Hildesheim: Olms, 1964), s.v. 'Pastorale'.

21 The first phrase of the second group (bars 66–73; *2a* in Table 5.3) is for instance rhythmically related to the second phrase of the first group (bars 13–20; *1b* in Table 5.3)

22 C. Rosen, *The Classical Style: Haydn, Mozart, Beethoven* (London: Faber & Faber, 1971), pp. 162–3. See also Webster, *Haydn's 'Farewell' Symphony*, pp. 236–49.

23 On connections (primarily harmonic) between movements in the works of Haydn see Webster, *Haydn's 'Farewell' Symphony*, esp. Pt. II, 'Cyclic Organization in Haydn's Instrumental Music'; E. Haimo, 'Remote Keys and Multi-movement Unity: Haydn in the 1790s', *Musical Quarterly* 74 (1990): 242–68; and *idem, Haydn's Symphonic Forms: Essays in Compositional Logic* (Oxford: Clarendon, 1995), pp. 274–6 and *passim*.

24 Another D major symphony, No. 53 ('Imperial', *c.*1778/9), was widely available in Paris and London in the early 1780s and was performed at the Bach–Abel Concerts in London in 1781 (see Landon, *Haydn at Eszterháza*, pp. 560–63) and Haydn included striking D major symphonies in his 'London' sets (Nos. 93, 96, 101 and 104).

25 Mozart's letter describing the impact of this gesture is quoted in Chapter 3.

26 See Webster, *Haydn's 'Farewell' Symphony*, p. 165.

27 On wit and comedy in instrumental music see Ratner, *Classic Music*, pp. 289, 386–96. See also the discussion of Symphony No. 83 in Chapter 7 below.

28 On Haydn's characteristic use of varied restatements of first themes as counter-statements in sonata-form keyboard movements, see my *Haydn's Keyboard Music: Studies in Performance Practice*, pp. 147–51; E. Sisman, *Haydn and the Classical Variation* (Cambridge, Mass.: Harvard University Press, 1993), pp. 95–108; *eadem*, 'Small and Expanded Forms: Koch's Model and Haydn's Music', *Musical Quarterly* 68 (1982): 444–75.

29 The harmonic character of this phrase, that is, in the dominant but without a clear articulation of the dominant until its end, is similar to bars 60–9 of 82/i. See note 14 above.

30 The insistence on the outline 8–5–3 in this cadence figure and the contrasting theme may be seen as related to the melodic outline in the Introduction, at bars 6–7, 8–9. K. Marx (in 'Über thematische Beziehungen in Haydns Londoner Symphonien', *Haydn-Studien* 4 (1976–80): 1–19) sees a significant relationship between bars 195–6 of the first movement and bars 15–6 of the second movement. For a critical assessment of 'thematicism' see Webster, *Haydn's 'Farewell' Symphony*, pp. 194–204; specifically on Marx, pp. 200–3.

31 The terminological problem in the use of the term 'monothematic' sonata form is mentioned in M. Fillion, 'Sonata-Exposition Procedures in Haydn's Keyboard Sonatas', in *Haydn Studies*, ed. J. P. Larsen *et al.*, p. 479.

32 See Sisman, 'Small and Expanded Forms', pp. 444–75.

33 Rosen, *Sonata Forms*, pp. 115–16. See also Haimo, *Haydn's Symphonic Forms*, pp. 198–201.

34 Koch, *Lexikon*, s.v. 'Capriccio'.

35 For discussions of Haydn's capriccio and fantasia movements see A. P. Brown, *Joseph Haydn's Keyboard Music: Sources and Style* (Bloomington: Indiana University Press, 1986), pp. 221–9; L. Somfai, *The Keyboard Sonatas of Joseph Haydn* (Chicago: University of Chicago Press, 1995), pp. 347–51; Sisman, *Classical Variation*, pp. 181–3 and *passim*; Webster, *Haydn's 'Farewell' Symphony*, pp. 294–300; F. Salzer, 'Haydn's Fantasia from the String Quartet, Opus 76, No. 6', *Music Forum* 4 (1976): 161–94.

36 On the influence of C. P. E. Bach on Haydn see Brown, *Joseph Haydn's Keyboard Music: Sources and Style*, pp. 203–29, and my *Haydn's Keyboard Music: Studies in Performance Practice*, pp. 167–95.

37 Quoted in Landon, *Haydn in England*, p. 134. See also Schroeder, *Haydn and the Enlightenment*, pp. 165–7, and H. C. R. Landon and D. W. Jones, *Haydn: His Life and Music* (London: Thames & Hudson, 1988), pp. 257–60.

38 Kant, *Kritik*, part 1, book 2, § 23–9, trans. Pluhar, pp. 97–140.

6 Convention and originality: Symphony No. 85

1 For detailed assessments of Symphonies Nos. 85 and 92 see Haimo, *Haydn's Symphonic Forms*, pp. 178–207, and C. Rosen, *Classical Style*, pp. 159–63. See also Webster, *Haydn's 'Farewell' Symphony*, pp. 167–73.

2 On the meaning of 'Classical' in music see especially Rosen, *Classical Style*, esp. pp. 19–29, 57–98; L. Finscher, 'Zum Begriff der Klassik in der Musik', *Deutsches Jahrbuch der Musikwissenschaft* 11 (1967): 9–34; idem, *Studien zur Geschichte des Streichquartetts*, vol. 1 (Kassel: Bärenreiter, 1974), pp. 238–75; Webster, *Haydn's 'Farewell' Symphony*, pp. 335–66.

3 T. S. Eliot, 'What is a Classic?' in *Selected Prose of T. S. Eliot*, ed. F. Kermode (London: Faber & Faber, 1975), pp. 115–31. Many of Eliot's criteria for a classic are closely echoed in Rosen's understanding of the Classical style in music, especially his emphasis on the maturity of language and his critical assessment of so-called *Sturm und Drang* works, which mirrors Eliot's claim of 'eccentricity' in works which precede a classic age.

4 Haimo, *Haydn's Symphonic Forms*, pp. 178–82; Landon, *Symphonies*, p. 409.

Haimo cites the analogies between bars 4–5 and 12–14, 31–3; 6–7 and 13–15; 3–4 and 20–2; 4–6 and 23–7.

5 In other ways the Recapitulation is also significantly different from the Exposition, for instance in the omission of one statement of the first theme (*1a*) and of the theme occurring at bars 62ff. (*2*). It is overall a drastic compression by comparison with the Exposition.

6 Sisman, 'Small and Expanded Forms', pp. 474–5 and *passim*; *eadem*, *Classical Variation*, pp. 99–100 and *passim*.

7 See J. P. Larsen, 'Sonata Form Problems', in *Handel, Haydn & the Viennese Classical Style*, trans. U. Krämer (Ann Arbor: UMI, 1988), pp. 276.

8 It is not inconceivable that Haydn calculated that the intertextual reference to the 'Farewell' Symphony would be recognised by Parisian audiences. The work was performed at the *Concert spirituel* and published in Paris in 1784 (see p. 103, note 20 above). On the impact of the 'Farewell' theme in Symphony No. 85 see Haimo, *Haydn's Symphonic Forms*, pp. 182–3. For a more general discussion of harmonic instability in the second half of expositions, particularly in the works of Beethoven, see B. Churgin, 'Harmonic and Tonal Instability in the Second Key Area of Classic Sonata Form', in *Convention in Eighteenth- and Nineteenth-Century Music: Essays in Honor of Leonard G. Ratner*, Festschrift Series No. 10, ed. W. J. Allanbrook, J. M. Levy, W. P. Mahrt (New York: Pendragon, 1992), pp. 23–57.

9 In Galeazzi's description of sonata form four methods of beginning the second part are presented and are distinguished primarily by the thematic material employed. Three recommendations begin with material 'transposed to the fifth of the [tonic] key'; the fourth recommendation has new material which for 'greatest surprise' begins in 'some related key'. See B. Churgin, 'Francesco Galeazzi's Description (1796) of Sonata Form', *Journal of the American Musicological Society* 21 (1968): 194–5.

10 See Rosen, *Sonata Forms*, pp. 250–62

11 Churgin, 'Galeazzi's Description of Sonata Form', p. 195.

12 J. La Rue, 'Bifocal Tonality in Haydn's Symphonies', in *Essays in Honor of Leonard G. Ratner*, ed. W. J. Allanbrook *et al.*, pp. 59–73. Rosen (*Sonata Forms*, pp. 255–60) also cites examples of this procedure in the works of Haydn and other composers, including an example from Michael Haydn which apparently pre-dates Haydn's Symphony No. 85.

13 Haimo, *Haydn's Symphonic Forms*, p. 194.

14 On the latter point see esp. *ibid.*, pp. 198–207.

15 *Ibid.*, pp. 180–2.

16 Rosen finds this play with structure 'delightful because it is so absurdly

gratuitous' (*Sonata Forms*, p. 116). See also Haimo, *Haydn's Symphonic Forms*, pp. 198–201.

17 See Haimo, *Haydn's Symphonic Forms*, pp. 203–7.

18 On this point see Sisman, *Classical Variation*, pp. 2–5.

19 Rosen, *Classical Style*, p. 435.

20 'As this movement displays features that we have already examined in some detail in previous analyses, we can dispense with a close analysis here' (Haimo, *Haydn's Symphonic Forms*, p. 195).

21 *Ibid.*, p. 195.

22 *Ibid.*, p. 195.

23 See Landon, *Haydn at Eszterháza*, p. 608. On the aesthetic significance of folksong in Haydn's symphonies see Schroeder, *Haydn and the Enlightenment*, pp. 68–71.

24 *Mercure de France*, 1 Jan. 1780, p. 33.

7 Irony and humour: Symphony No. 83

1 Schroeder, *Haydn and the Enlightenment*, p. 68.

2 On Haydn's *Sturm und Drang* style see esp. Landon, *Haydn at Eszterháza*, pp. 266–84; B. S. Brook, '*Sturm und Drang* and the Romantic Period in Music', *Studies in Romanticism* 9 (1970): 269–84; R. L. Todd, 'Joseph Haydn and the *Sturm und Drang*: A Revaluation', *Music Review* 41 (1980): 172–96.

3 On these characteristics in the first movement of Symphony No. 83 see esp. Schroeder, *Haydn and the Enlightenment*, pp. 85–7.

4 *Ibid.*, pp. 85–6.

5 The *Rutscher* theme is here similar in function to the first theme in the dominant in Symphony No. 82/i. See above Chapter 5, note 14.

6 Cf. Schroeder's discussion of the contrast of serious and comic themes in Symphony No. 80 (*Haydn and the Enlightenment*, pp. 82–3).

7 *Ibid.*, pp. 85–7.

8 See B. Moyer, '*Ombra* and Fantasia in Late Eighteenth-Century Theory and Practice', in *Essays in Honor of Leonard G. Ratner*, ed. W. J. Allanbrook *et al.*, pp. 283–306.

9 Landon, *Haydn at Eszterháza*, p. 610.

10 Michaelis, 'The Beautiful and the Sublime in Music', trans. in Le Huray and Day, *Music and Aesthetics*, pp. 202–3.

11 Trans. in Le Huray and Day, *Music and Aesthetics*, p. 205. For discussions of humour in music see esp. G. A. Wheelock, *Haydn's Ingenious Jesting with Art:*

Contexts of Musical Wit and Humor (New York: Schirmer, 1992), and S. E. Paul, 'Wit, Comedy, and Humour in the Instrumental Music of Franz Joseph Haydn' (Ph.D. diss., Cambridge University, 1980).

12 Trans. in Le Huray and Day, *Music and Aesthetics*, p. 204.

13 *Ibid.*, p. 205.

14 For Kant it is the 'free play' of the imagination which characterised aesthetic judgement, and 'this state of free play of the cognitive powers, accompanying a presentation by which an object is given, must be universally communicable' (*Kritik*, part 1, book 1, § 9, trans. Pluhar, p. 62)

15 Voltaire, *Philosophical Dictionary*, quoted in J. L. Schwartz, 'Periodicity and Passion in the First Movement of Haydn's "Farewell" Symphony', in *Essays in Honor of Jan La Rue*, ed. E. K. Wolf and E. Roesner (Madison: A–R Editions, 1990), pp. 335–6.

16 See for instance M. E. Bonds, 'Haydn, Laurence Sterne, and the Origins of Musical Irony', *Journal of the American Musicological Society* 44 (1991), pp. 83–4. Famously, Charles Burney referred to the same criticisms (*A General History of Music* (London, 1776–89), vol. 4, p. 601).

17 Bonds, 'Haydn, Laurence Sterne, and the Origins of Musical Irony', pp. 57–91, esp. 63–78.

18 See, for instance, Webster's discussion of the D major interlude in the first movement of the 'Farewell' Symphony as ironic (*Haydn's 'Farewell' Symphony*, pp. 39–45).

19 See K. Wheeler, *German Aesthetic and Literary Criticism: The Romantic Ironists and Goethe* (Cambridge: Cambridge University Press, 1984).

20 Landon, *Haydn at Eszterháza*, p. 610.

21 'Über Goethes *Meister*' (1798), trans. in Wheeler, *German Aesthetic and Literary Criticism*, p. 64.

8 The refinement of popular taste: Symphonies Nos. 84 and 87

1 Letter of 2 August 1787; *CCLN*, p. 68.

2 See J. P. Larsen, 'On the Importance of the "Mannheim School"' in *Handel, Haydn & the Viennese Classical Style*, pp. 264–5.

3 Haydn's use of the *Orchesterwalzer* in Symphony No. 1 (pre-1759) has been described by Landon as a 'musical red herring' in view of the irrelevance of the Mannheim influence on Haydn's early works (Landon, *Haydn: Chronicle & Works*, vol. 1, *Haydn: The Early Years* (London: Thames & Hudson, 1980) p. 283; see also p. 112).

4 See Ratner, *Classic Music*, pp. 19, 27–8; G. Pestelli, *The Age of Mozart and*

Beethoven, trans. E. Cross (Cambridge: Cambridge University Press, 1984), p. 136.

5 See Sisman, *Classical Variation*, pp. 164–95 *passim* . Cf. Symphonies Nos. 82/ii and 85/ii.

6 The cadenza in Symphony No. 84/ii is an integrated cadenza in the sense that it is linked thematically to the movement *per se* (see P. Whitmore, *Unpremeditated Art: The Cadenza in the Classical Keyboard Concerto* (Oxford: Clarendon, 1991), pp. 30–1). Notwithstanding their multi-voiced scoring, the cadenzas in Symphonies Nos. 87/ii and 84/ii both broadly follow procedures observable in eighteenth-century duet cadenzas (*ibid.*, pp. 32–4).

7 Cf. Symphony No. 85/ii (bars 23–44) and the *minore* theme and its first variation in the double-variation set of Symphony No. 82 (bars 33–60, 101–28).

Select bibliography

Allanbrook, W. J., J. M. Levy, W. P. Mahrt, eds., *Convention in Eighteenth- and Nineteenth-Century Music: Essays in Honor of Leonard G. Ratner*, Festschrift Series No. 10 (New York: Pendragon, 1992).

Anderson, E., ed., *The Letters of Mozart and His Family*, 2nd edn, 2 vols. (London: Macmillan, 1966).

Bonds, M. E., 'Haydn, Laurence Sterne, and the Origins of Musical Irony', *Journal of the American Musicological Society* 44 (1991): 57–91.

Brenet, M., *Les Concerts en France sous l'ancien régime* (Paris, 1900; repr., New York: Da Capo, 1970).

Brook, B., *La Symphonie française dans la seconde moitié du XVIII⁰ siècle*, 2 vols. (Paris: Institut de Musicologie de l'Université de Paris, 1962).

'Sturm und Drang and the Romantic Period in Music', *Studies in Romanticism* 9 (1970): 269–84.

Brown, A. P., *Joseph Haydn's Keyboard Music: Sources and Style* (Bloomington: Indiana University Press, 1986).

Burney, C., *A General History of Music*, 4 vols. (London, 1776–89).

Charlton, D. G., *New Images of the Natural in France: A Study in European Cultural History, 1750–1800* (Cambridge: Cambridge University Press, 1984).

Churgin, B., 'Francesco Galeazzi's Description (1796) of Sonata Form', *Journal of the American Musicological Society* 21 (1968): 181–99.

'Harmonic and Tonal Instability in the Second Key Area of Classic Sonata Form', in *Essays in Honor of Leonard G. Ratner*, ed. W. J. Allanbrook *et al.*, pp. 23–57.

Dahlhaus, C., *Foundations of Music History*, trans. J. B. Robinson (Cambridge: Cambridge University Press, 1983).

'What is Developing Variation?' in *Schoenberg and the New Music*, trans. D. Puffett and A. Clayton (Cambridge, 1987), pp. 128–33.

The Idea of Absolute Music, trans. R. Lustig (Chicago: University of Chicago Press, 1989).

Ludwig van Beethoven: Approaches to His Music, trans. M. Whittall (Oxford: Clarendon Press, 1991).

Eliot, T. S., 'What is a Classic?' in *Selected Prose of T. S. Eliot*, ed. F. Kermode (London: Faber & Faber, 1975), pp. 115–31.

Epstein, D., *Beyond Orpheus: Studies in Musical Structure* (Oxford: Oxford University Press, 1987).

Fillion, M., 'Sonata-Exposition Procedures in Haydn's Keyboard Sonatas', in *Haydn Studies*, ed. J. P. Larsen *et al.*, pp. 475–81.

Finscher, L., ' Zum Begriff der Klassik in der Musik', *Deutsches Jahrbuch der Musikwissenschaft* 11 (1967): 9–34.

Studien zur Geschichte des Streichquartetts, vol. 1 (Kassel: Bärenreiter, 1974).

Fisher, S. C., 'Sonata Procedures in Haydn's Symphonic Rondo Finales of the 1770s', in *Haydn Studies*, ed. J. P. Larsen *et al.*, pp. 481–7.

Fubini, E., *History of Music Aesthetics*, trans. M. Hatwell (London: Macmillan, 1990).

Music and Culture in Eighteenth-Century Europe: A Source Book, ed. B. Blackburn (Chicago: University of Chicago Press, 1994).

Gay, P., *The Enlightenment: An Interpretation*, 2 vols. (New York: Vintage, 1966, 1969).

Gluck, C. W. von, 'Lettre de M. le Chevalier Gluck, sur la musique', *Mercure de France*, Feb. 1773, p. 182; trans. in Le Huray and Day, *Music and Aesthetics*, p. 116.

Griesinger, G. A., *Biographische Notizen über Joseph Haydn*, trans. V. Gotwals in *Joseph Haydn: Eighteenth-Century Gentleman and Genius* (Madison: University of Wisconsin Press, 1963).

Haimo, E., 'Remote Keys and Multi-movement Unity: Haydn in the 1790s', *Musical Quarterly* 74 (1990): 242–68.

Haydn's Symphonic Forms: Essays in Compositional Logic (Oxford: Clarendon, 1995).

Harrison. B., *Haydn's Keyboard Music: Studies in Performance Practice* (Oxford: Clarendon, 1997).

Hoboken, A. van, *Joseph Haydn: Thematisch-bibliographisches Werkverzeichnis*, 3 vols. (Mainz: Schott, 1957–78).

Isherwood, R., 'The Third War of the Musical Enlightenment', *Studies in Eighteenth-Century Culture* 4, ed. H. Pagliaro (Madison: University of Wisconsin Press, 1975), pp. 223–45.

Johnson, J. H., *Listening in Paris: A Cultural History* (Berkeley: University of California Press, 1995).

'Beethoven and the Birth of Romantic Musical Experience in France', *19th-Century Music* 15 (1991): 23–35.

Jordanova, L., ed., *Languages of Nature: Critical Essays on Science and Literature* (London: Free Association Books, 1986).

Kant, I., *Kritik der Urtheilskraft* (Berlin, 1790), trans. W. Pluhar (Indianapolis: Hackett, 1987).

Koch, H. C., *Musikalisches Lexikon* (Frankfurt, 1802; facsimile repr., Hildesheim: Olms, 1964).

Landon, H. C. R., *The Symphonies of Joseph Haydn* (London: Universal & Rockliff, 1955).

ed., *The Collected Correspondence and London Notebooks of Joseph Haydn* (London: Barrie & Rockliff, 1959).

Haydn: Chronicle and Works, 5 vols. (London: Thames & Hudson, 1976–80).

and D. W. Jones, *Haydn: His Life and Music* (London: Thames & Hudson, 1988).

Larsen, J. P., 'Sonata Form Problems', in *Handel, Haydn & the Viennese Classical Style*, trans. U. Krämer (Ann Arbor: UMI, 1988), pp. 269–79.

'On the Importance of the "Mannheim School"', in *Handel, Haydn & the Viennese Classical Style*, pp. 263–8.

H. Serwer, J. Webster, eds., *Haydn Studies: Proceedings of the International Haydn Conference, Washington, D. C., 1975* (New York: Norton, 1981).

La Rue, J. 'Symphony', in *The New Grove Dictionary of Music and Musicians*, ed. S. Sadie (London: Macmillan, 1980).

'Bifocal Tonality in Haydn's Symphonies', in *Essays in Honor of Leonard G. Ratner*, ed. W. J. Allanbrook *et al.*, pp. 59–73.

Launay, D., ed., *La Querelle des Bouffons: Texte des pamphlets avec introduction, commentaires, et index*, 3 vols. (Geneva: Minkoff, 1973).

Le Huray, P., and J. Day, *Music and Aesthetics in the Eighteenth and Early-Nineteenth Centuries*, abridged edn (Cambridge: Cambridge University Press, 1988).

Lippman, E., *A History of Western Musical Aesthetics* (Lincoln: University of Nebraska Press, 1992).

Lowinsky, E., 'Taste, Style, and Ideology in Eighteenth-Century Music', in *Aspects of the Eighteenth Century*, ed. E. Wasserman (Baltimore: Johns Hopkins University Press, 1965), pp. 163–205.

Marx, K., 'Über thematische Beziehungen in Haydns Londoner Symphonien', *Haydn-Studien* 4 (1976–80): 1–19.

Mongrédien, J., 'Paris: The End of the Ancien Régime', in *Man & Music: The Classical Era*, ed. N. Zaslaw (London: Macmillan, 1989).

Moyer, B., '*Ombra* and Fantasia in Late Eighteenth-Century Theory and Practice', in *Essays in Honor of Leonard G. Ratner*, ed. W. J. Allanbrook *et al.*, pp. 283–306.

Neubauer, J., *The Emancipation of Music from Language: Departures from*

Mimesis in Eighteenth-Century Aesthetics (New Haven: Yale University Press, 1986).

Paul, S. E. 'Wit, Comedy, and Humour in the Instrumental Music of Franz Joseph Haydn' (Ph.D. diss., Cambridge University, 1980).

Pestelli, G., *The Age of Mozart and Beethoven*, trans. E. Cross (Cambridge: Cambridge University Press, 1984).

Pierre, C. *Histoire du Concert spirituel, 1725–1790* (Paris: Société Française de Musicologie, 1975).

Quoy-Bodin, J.-L., 'L'Orchestre de la Société Olympique en 1786', *Revue de musicologie* 70 (1984): 95–107.

Ratner, L., *Classic Music: Expression, Form, and Style* (New York: Schirmer, 1980).

Rosen, C., *The Classical Style: Haydn, Mozart, Beethoven* (London: Faber & Faber, 1971).

Sonata Forms (New York: Norton, 1980).

Rousseau, J.-J., *Dictionnaire de musique* (Paris, 1768).

Ruiter, J. de, *Der Charakterbegriff in der Musik: Studien zur deutschen Ästhetik der Instrumentalmusik, 1740–1850*, Beihefte zum Archiv für Musikwissenschaft, 29 (Stuttgart: Steiner, 1989).

Salzer, F., 'Haydn's Fantasia from the String Quartet, Opus 76, No. 6', *Music Forum* 4 (1976): 161–94.

Schroeder, D., *Haydn and the Enlightenment: The Late Symphonies and Their Audience* (Oxford: Clarendon, 1990).

Schulz, J. A. P., 'Symphonie', in J. G. Sulzer, *Allgemeine Theorie der schönen Künste* (Leipzig, 1771–4; facsimile of 2nd edn, Hildesheim: Olms, 1994), vol. 4, pp. 478–9.

Schwartz, J. L., 'Periodicity and Passion in the First Movement of Haydn's "Farewell" Symphony', in *Studies in Musical Sources and Style: Essays in Honor of Jan La Rue*, eds. E. K. Wolf and E. Roesner (Madison: A-R Editions, 1990), pp. 293–338.

Sisman, E., 'Haydn's Hybrid Variations', in *Haydn Studies*, ed. J. P. Larsen *et al.*, pp. 509–15.

'Small and Expanded Forms: Koch's Model and Haydn's Music', *Musical Quarterly* 68 (1982): 444–75.

Mozart: The 'Jupiter' Symphony (Cambridge: Cambridge University Press, 1993).

Haydn and the Classical Variation (Cambridge, Mass.: Harvard University Press, 1993).

Somfai, L., *The Keyboard Sonatas of Joseph Haydn* (Chicago: University of Chicago Press, 1995).

Steblin, R., *History of Key Characteristics in the Eighteenth and Early Nineteenth Centuries* (Ann Arbor: UMI, 1983).

Sulzer, J. G., *Allgemeine Theorie der schönen Künste* (Leipzig, 1771–4; facsimile of 2nd edn, Hildesheim: Olms, 1994).

Todd, R. L., 'Joseph Haydn and the *Sturm und Drang*: A Revaluation', *Music Review* 41 (1980): 172–96.

Verba, C., *Music and the French Enlightenment: Reconstruction of a Dialogue 1750–1764* (Oxford: Oxford University Press, 1993).

Voltaire, *Philosophical Dictionary*, trans. T. Besterman (London: Penguin, 1972).

Walter, H. ed., *Joseph Haydn: Konzerte für Klavier (Cembalo) und Orchester*, JHW, XV,2 (Munich: Henle, 1983).

Weber, W., 'Learned and General Musical Taste in Eighteenth-Century France', *Past and Present* 89 (1980): 58–85.

'The Contemporaneity of Eighteenth-Century Musical Taste', *Musical Quarterly* 70 (1984): 175–94.

Webster, J., 'When Did Haydn Begin to Write "Beautiful" Melodies?' in *Haydn Studies*, ed. J. P. Larsen *et al.*, pp. 385–8.

Haydn's "Farewell" Symphony and the Idea of Classical Style (Cambridge: Cambridge University Press, 1991).

Wheeler, K., *German Aesthetic and Literary Criticism: The Romantic Ironists and Goethe* (Cambridge: Cambridge University Press, 1984).

Wheelock, G. A., *Haydn's Ingenious Jesting with Art: Contexts of Musical Wit and Humor* (New York: Schirmer, 1992).

Whitmore, P., *Unpremeditated Art: The Cadenza in the Classical Keyboard Concerto* (Oxford: Clarendon, 1991).

Wolf, E. K., 'The Recapitulations in Haydn's London Symphonies', *Musical Quarterly* 52 (1966): 71–89.

Zaslaw, N., 'Mozart's Paris Symphonies', *Musical Times* 119 (1978): 753–7.

Mozart's Symphonies: Context, Performance Practice, Reception (Oxford: Oxford University Press, 1989).

ed. *Man & Music: The Classical Era* (London: Macmillan, 1989).

Index